THE FAMILY RECOVERY PROGRAM

THE FAMILY RECOVERY PROGRAM

A Professional's Guide

Second Edition

by Joseph Nowinski, Ph.D.

HAZELDEN®

Hazelden
Center City, Minnesota 55012
hazelden.org

First edition published 1999. Second edition published by Hazelden 2011

Printed in the United States of America

ISBN: 978-1-61649-107-9

Editor's note
The names, details, and circumstances may have been changed to protect the privacy of those mentioned in this publication.

This publication is not intended as a substitute for the advice of health care professionals.

Cover design by Theresa Jaeger Gedig
Interior design and typesetting by David Farr, ImageSmythe

How to Access the Resources on the CD-ROM

The Family Recovery Program CD-ROM contains electronic versions of the checklists and handouts referred to in this manual for ease of reproducing. All of these resources are in PDF format and can be accessed using Adobe Reader. If you do not have Adobe Reader, you can download it for free at www.adobe.com.

Whenever you see this icon in this guide, this means the needed resource is on the CD-ROM.

To access these resources, put the disk in your computer's CD-ROM player. Open your version of Adobe Reader. Then open the documents by finding them on your CD-ROM drive. These resources cannot be modified, but they may be printed for use without concern for copyright infringement.

See page 230 for a list of the resources on the CD-ROM.

For Terri

Contents

Foreword

Alcoholism is not a spectator sport. Everyone gets to play. It is possible for every symptom of addiction to be present in nonaddicted family members, without them ever swallowing a drink of alcohol or taking an illegal drug. Al-Anon came into existence partly because the wives of alcoholics noticed that while their husbands' lives were improving with the help of Alcoholics Anonymous (AA), their own lives were not. They thought if they practiced the Twelve Steps of AA themselves, their own lives might improve too. They were right.

An addiction treatment program or an addiction treatment process that only treats the substance abuser is treating less than half the problem. It is often said that addiction is a family disease. In the absence of true family recovery, the substance abuser is less likely to attain and maintain his or her own recovery.

Hazelden has operated a Family Program since 1966 that welcomes family members and friends of alcoholics and addicts for a short stay on campus. There they learn about the disease of addiction, about the effects of addiction on the family, and about important adaptations they can make themselves to promote and sustain family-wide recovery. At Hazelden they learn the concepts of acceptance, caring detachment, surrender to a Higher Power, and the adoption of an Al-Anon or Nar-Anon way of life.

These same life-changing principles compose the core of this book, providing readers with a road map to Twelve Step family recovery. Readers who have no background in this type of family recovery will discover enough about Al-Anon and Nar-Anon to introduce these fellowships to their clients. Those who are familiar with these programs will find the book a welcome refresher as well as a resource they can share with clients who seek to embark on a journey of family recovery.

This book has unswerving accuracy in portraying Al-Anon and Nar-Anon—so much so, that it is tempting to simply give it to the suffering family member and say, "Here it is; do this." However, Al-Anon and Nar-Anon are much more than programs based on a set of Twelve Steps to be memorized, a set of slogans, or even a twelve-week study group. They are programs for changing one's way of life to overcome the deleterious effects of a loved one's addiction. Families ultimately need to immerse themselves in the Al-Anon and Nar-Anon way of life, with meetings, speakers, and appropriate books; by working the Twelve Steps; and by learning to think from an Al-Anon or Nar-Anon perspective. This book will help them do so.

Moving from a state of confusion to a state of focused serenity often requires facilitation. In Al-Anon and Nar-Anon, this is provided by sponsors and trusted friends. This book outlines a plan for a trusted therapist to do the same kind of facilitation in a thorough and structured plan of twelve sessions, scheduled over a period of up to six months.

Dr. Nowinski provides addiction professionals (clinicians, social workers, clinical psychologists, family therapists, and substance abuse counselors) with theoretical background and specific advice so they can understand the process of Twelve Step family recovery well enough to incorporate it into their own practices and teach it to others. Session guidelines are included for easy reference, and the in-depth facilitator guide, along with helpful treatment notes and advice for troubleshooting challenging situations, provide facilitators with what they need to foster family recovery.

Ultimately, this book will have been successful when the family no longer needs professional guidance and instead finds its own recovery through Al-Anon or Nar-Anon, whether or not the identified addict or alcoholic has moved on in his or her recovery in Alcoholics Anonymous or Narcotics Anonymous.

John A. MacDougall, M.Div., D.Min.
Director, Hazelden Family Program
Center City, Minnesota

Preface to the Second Edition

Chronic substance abuse can have devastating effects on families. Although concerned others are often motivated to get help in persuading the substance abuser to seek treatment, they are often in dire need of help themselves. Numerous negative effects of ongoing substance abuse on family members have been documented. These negative effects include declines in psychological and social adjustment, deterioration in relationships, loss of family cohesion, and increased interpersonal conflict, including domestic violence.[1] Other experts have found family members of chronic substance abusers to be significantly stressed[2] and to experience greater degrees of depression and physical symptoms, as well as decreased self-confidence, as compared to matched control groups.[3] It is generally recognized then that the emotional, spiritual, and physical health of significant others is seriously compromised by a loved one's addiction.[4] These individuals have significant clinical needs that, unfortunately, may be overlooked in the effort to prompt the substance abuser to seek help. Considering that as many as 80 percent of individuals suffering from addiction may be in denial of the problem and/or unmotivated to change,[5] failure to address the very real needs of significant others poses an ongoing threat to the mental health of literally millions of individuals.

Given these realities, the clinician faces a twofold challenge: to respond to the significant other's desire for help in dealing with the substance abuser, and to tend to the mental and physical health of the significant other. In short, the implied therapeutic agenda is complex. The goal of the Family Recovery Program (FRP) as it is presented in this book, however, is clear: to help loved ones change in ways that will improve their own health and well-being. A secondary effect of those changes—a movement away from enabling toward caring detachment—could be that the substance abuser begins to contemplate his or her addiction problem and consider necessary life changes. This latter effect often emerges as a result of the restructured relationship between a significant other and the substance abuser.

This book will be useful to both experienced clinicians and those who are training to be clinical social workers, clinical psychologists, family therapists, and substance abuse counselors. The FRP has been used by all of these groups. Experienced clinicians will find it useful in extending their range of clinical competence with respect to the Twelve Step model of addiction as it pertains to working with family members and other loved ones of substance abusers. Those in training will find it a helpful guide, allowing them to focus treatment.

This second edition includes a new addition: Family Recovery Program Session Guidelines. These guidelines, which can be reproduced using the included CD-ROM, are designed to be a convenient way for therapists to implement the FRP in therapy sessions. Therapists have found such guidelines useful. A second use for the guidelines is as a tool for clinical supervision and for monitoring treatment fidelity. In this case, an observer uses the session guidelines to determine how well a therapist adheres to the treatment protocol.

This treatment program is highly structured and seeks to help the clinician achieve fairly specific and delineated goals. It has been field-tested in clinical trials with significant others of alcohol and drug abusers.[6] Spouses and cohabiting partners, parents, siblings, and other loved ones of substance abusers—including grandparents and adult children—have all been treated using the program described here. It has not been used with minor children of substance abusers. The case examples presented are based on clinical cases drawn largely from these trials, supplemented by the author's own clinical experience.

It goes without saying that the family is a system of interdependent relationships. It is, therefore, reasonable to assume that any significant change in one member of a family will inevitably change his or her relationships with all others, affecting the entire family system. In the course of implementing the FRP, we have found this to be true. That is not to say that other approaches are not effective. The approach presented here, however, is most compatible with the Twelve Step model of recovery. It is intended to be implemented in a relatively brief span of time (ten to twelve sessions). As such, it is particularly useful to those clinicians who must provide care in a managed-care environment. In that environment, allocation of services is closely monitored and contingent on setting specific therapeutic goals and objectives, and third-party payers advocate the use of self-help groups, such as Alcoholics Anonymous (AA) and Al-Anon, as adjuncts to formal treatment.

Acknowledgments

I would like to acknowledge a number of people whose support and input contributed substantially to this work. Bill Miller and Bob Meyers of the Center for Alcoholism, Substance Abuse, and Addictions of the University of New Mexico, offered me the opportunity to develop this treatment program for inclusion in their studies of unilateral intervention with significant others of substance abusers. I am grateful for that opportunity.

My first exposure to the Twelve Step approach to family recovery took place when I participated in the Family Program at the Hazelden Foundation as a Professional in Residence. It was in that context that I first witnessed the power of caring detachment in changing individuals and families.

Patricia Owen of the Hazelden Foundation was generous in reading a draft of the manuscript and provided very constructive feedback that was incorporated into the final draft. Lastly, thanks to my loyal editor, Richard Solly, for his unflagging support.

Part 1 || Principles of Twelve Step Family Recovery

Chapter 1 || How It Works

The fellowships of Al-Anon and Nar-Anon apply the principles and steps of Twelve Step recovery as developed originally by Alcoholics Anonymous (AA) and later adopted by Narcotics Anonymous (NA) to concerned significant others[1] of individuals with alcohol or other psychoactive substance use disorders. This includes spouses or cohabiting partners, parents, children, and other close relations and loved ones of substance abusers. The philosophical connection between Al-Anon and AA is reflected in the fact that the Twelve Steps that guide each fellowship are identical.

Addiction and codependence are viewed by AA and by Al-Anon (and NA and Nar-Anon) as parallel processes characterized by *progressive loss of control* over psychoactive substance use. For the addict or alcoholic, it is use of the actual substance over which she or he progressively loses control; for the codependent, it is the ability to influence the substance abuser's behavior (to get him or her to stop drinking or using other drugs) that one loses control over. *(Note: For brevity, I will at times use the term* substance abuser *to refer to alcoholics as well as those addicted to other psychoactive substances.)* For the substance abuser and the concerned significant other alike, life becomes increasingly unmanageable as a direct result of substance abuse. Moreover, addiction gradually erodes not just the substance abuser—physically, psychologically, and spiritually—but can have the very same effect on those closest to the substance abuser. Recovery for both the substance abuser and the codependent involves a process of healing in each of these three areas. Clinicians who are approached by significant others seeking help in convincing the substance abuser to seek treatment need to appreciate the codependent's need for healing as well.

The basic principles that guide the Twelve Step fellowships of Al-Anon and Nar-Anon are

- *acceptance* of the loss of control over the substance abuser,
- *surrender* to some Higher Power as an entity other than individual willpower in which to place one's hope and faith, and

- a *decision* to pursue the Twelve Step program of personal growth and renewal.

Just as AA states that alcoholics must let go of the illusion that they can successfully and reliably moderate drinking through willpower alone, Al-Anon and Nar-Anon assert that loved ones must also let go of any illusion that they can stop or control another person's drinking or drug use through their own willpower alone. Instead, these fellowships advocate that loved ones modify their own attitudes and behaviors in ways that promote their own physical, spiritual, and mental health. They believe that the substance abuser must come to make his or her own decision to change. The essence of the Al-Anon message, therefore, is that the best way to effect change in another is not to coerce, cajole, or threaten, but rather *to change one's own behavior in relation to that person.*

Al-Anon and Nar-Anon could be seen as taking a paradoxical position on change: That fewer efforts to *control* a problem drinker or drug user and more efforts to modify the dynamics of the substance abuser–codependent relationship in the direction of *caring detachment* as described herein is more likely in the long run to lead a substance abuser to come to terms with his or her problem. In its approach to addiction, the Twelve Step model does much to relieve loved ones of the chronic stress, guilt, and shame associated with feeling responsible for getting a substance abuser to change (and perhaps for having caused the problem in the first place).

In Al-Anon and Nar-Anon, concerned significant others are advised to *detach:* to cease engaging in all those behaviors that (often inadvertently) *enable* the substance abuser to continue using and, therefore, have the unintended effect of supporting the status quo. In part, detaching involves allowing the substance abuser to experience the natural consequences of addiction without the codependent attempting to mitigate or minimize them. A simple rule derives from this advice: By enabling the substance abuser, the codependent unwittingly undermines any motivation for change, whereas through detaching, the codependent may actually enhance motivation for change. Still, enhancing that motivation is not the main goal of these fellowships; rather, it is to support the codependent's efforts to take care of himself or herself physically, psychologically, and spiritually.

Another way to look at detaching and its effects is in terms of the *transtheoretical* model of change.[2] According to this theory, behavioral change is dependent on circumstances becoming uncomfortable enough for the individual first to perceive cause-effect relationships (e.g., between drinking and negative consequences), then to make a decision to change, then to take specific action toward changing, and last, to maintain that change. Whereas enabling has the unintended effect of mitigating the consequences of addiction (and therefore allowing the substance abuser to remain in a "precontemplative" state of denial), detaching exposes the substance abuser to consequences that could lead him or her to "contemplate" having a problem and to possibly decide that action is needed.

In AA and NA, the substance abuser, by reflecting on the negative consequences of substance abuse on his or her own life (in part through listening to and identifying with others' stories and then telling his or her own), is helped to gradually move from *denial* of any problem toward *acceptance* that substance abuse has, in fact, rendered his or her life increasingly unmanageable. The next step, then, becomes one of *action*: The substance abuser recognizes the need to give up illusions of moderation as a viable goal and to *surrender* instead to abstinence from substance use as a long-term goal and to active participation in the fellowship of AA or NA (or both) as a means to that end.

Within Twelve Step fellowships, substance abusers are continually encouraged to turn to spirituality (faith and hope) to maintain motivation in the face of relapses (slips) or a history of failure and to use the resources within these fellowships for practical advice and support to maintain abstinence "one day at a time." Although their shared goal is abstinence, Twelve Step fellowships are not so naïve as to expect recovery to be a single event; rather, recovery is regarded as a *process* that is often marked by slips. For that reason, a single day of sobriety—a decision to "not drink or use today"—is recognized, just as is an anniversary of sobriety.

This process is the core theme of the stories that make up the bulk of the "big books" and that are also a central focus of AA and NA meetings.[3] By going to meetings, listening, and identifying, many substance abusers have found their way from addiction to recovery.

The process through which alcoholics move from denial to acceptance is succinctly summarized in chapter 8 of *Alcoholics Anonymous*.[4] In principle, it applies to drug addicts just as well. Although somewhat dated in its language (and unfortunately titled "To Wives," because few AA members were female at the time it was written), it nonetheless describes with remarkable clarity what is essentially a three-stage process that all substance abusers go through:

- Stage One: Your husband may be only a heavy drinker. . . . It may be slowing him up mentally and physically, but he does not see it. . . . He is positive he can handle his liquor . . .[5]
- Stage Two: Your husband is showing lack of control . . . He often gets entirely out of hand when drinking. He admits this is true, but is positive that he will do better.[6]
- Stage Three: His friends have slipped away, his home is a near-wreck and he cannot hold a position. . . . He admits he cannot drink like other people, but does not see why. He clings to the notion that he will yet find a way to do so. He may have come to the point where he desperately wants to stop but cannot.[7]

The last stage described—of wanting to stop but being unable to—is the point at which many substance abusers finally and reluctantly admit to themselves and others that they have a problem. It is only at this point that many make their first appearance at an AA or an NA meeting. This admission—of personal failure over the long run to control alcohol or drug use and the unmanageability that has been the result—is crucial, for it sets the stage for the alcoholic or addict to be open, first, to the need for abstinence and, second, to the advice of others on how to achieve it. The primary vehicle for this openness is the stories that the alcoholic or addict hears at meetings.

Note: The single term meeting *is used here to refer to any Twelve Step fellowship meeting, including* AA, NA, *Al-Anon, and Nar-Anon.*

The key to recovery, then, lies in a willingness to admit to the inadequacy of one's personal willpower in effectively controlling alcohol or drug use and to place one's faith instead in the collective wisdom and interpersonal resources of a Twelve Step fellowship. The format of the personal stories told at AA, NA, and other Twelve Step meetings—how it was, what happened, how it is now—represents what has been called a "core story" of personal transformation founded on spiritual faith and bonding to the fellowship.[8] It stands as a stark counterpoint to what has been called "radical individualism"[9] (or "self-will run riot" as Bill Wilson put it[10]) in which personal willpower is seen as being more potent than either faith or group support. The core story of AA is a heroic one in contrast to the story of gradual self-immolation that is the story of the addiction process. It is also a story that advocates the strength of fellowship over the strength of individual willpower as a means of achieving and sustaining change.

Storytelling as a tradition and ritual serves to keep the memory of addiction and its consequences from fading and repeatedly affirms each member's decision to surrender to the fellowship and to the Twelve Steps as a pathway to spiritual renewal and character growth.

Al-Anon and Nar-Anon

Al-Anon and Nar-Anon are based in a belief that "letting go" of the substance abuser—by learning to *detach* instead of *enable*—is the best way to heal the deleterious effects that addiction has on loved ones, *and* potentially to motivate the substance abuser to progress through the stages of awareness, decision, and action in the change process. By enabling the substance abuser, the codependent unwittingly supports the status quo. One common effect of enabling is to insulate the substance abuser from facing the true and natural consequences of his or her substance abuse. Enabling invariably moderates these consequences and thereby undermines the change process. In contrast, by learning to detach in a caring way, the codependent simultaneously takes care of himself or herself while helping to expose the substance abuser to the true unmanageability that addiction creates, thereby promoting change.

Al-Anon can be described as a fellowship that exists for the benefit of the *affected*: for those significant others whose lives—whose mental, spiritual, and physical health—have been affected negatively as a consequence of being in a close relationship with an addict or alcoholic.[11] In addition to Al-Anon, which welcomes all those whose lives are affected by alcohol, Alateen is a fellowship specifically for the children of alcoholics. Similarly, Nar-Anon is a fellowship that is open to significant others of drug addicts.

Despite their implied belief that caring detachment will ultimately prove more successful than enabling to get alcoholics and addicts sober, all of these fellowships exist first and foremost not so much to motivate alcoholics or addicts as for the support and renewal of loved ones who have been negatively affected by addiction. Depression born of chronic frustration and failure (to get the alcoholic or addict to stop), compounded by feelings of shame or guilt (over possibly being responsible), and anxiety (over what might happen next) are some of the emotional and spiritual burdens that are commonly brought to Al-Anon and Nar-Anon. Families typically spiral downward into dysfunction as they unravel in the face of addiction. Al-Anon and Nar-Anon are fellowships in which such problems can be talked about openly, where emotional wounds can be healed, and where personal growth can be renewed. *This is so, regardless of whether or not the substance abuser chooses recovery over addiction.*

AA and NA were founded on the idea that alcoholics and drug addicts must eventually make the decision on their own to stop trying to control their drinking and drugging through willpower and, instead, accept the necessity to abstain (with the advice and support of fellow recovering substance abusers). Al-Anon and Nar-Anon represent the complement of this. These fellowships recognize that codependents often need help accepting their own powerlessness over the substance abuser and that they also need support in learning to detach (as opposed to enabling the substance abuser). Al-Anon and Nar-Anon's primary assumptions are as follows:

- *Loss of Control:* Just as the substance abuser becomes progressively more powerless to effectively moderate drinking or using other drugs as he or she moves from social use through habitual use toward eventual compulsive use, so is the codependent progressively more powerless with respect to getting the substance abuser to stop. The codependent cannot prevent the alcoholic from drinking or the addict from using, but it may take a long time to truly accept this fact.[12]
- *Faith:* Because the codependent is, in fact, powerless (over addiction), she or he needs to "turn over" the fate of the substance abuser to a Higher Power—in effect, to stop efforts to control the behavior of the substance abuser or shield him or her from negative consequences of use. Instead, according to Al-Anon, codependents need to begin attending to their own health and well-being.[13] Just as the substance abuser can harbor despair about the chances for success, so can the codependent feel hopeless and helpless. The emphasis on faith within Twelve Step fellowships relates directly to this problem. Hopelessness undermines motivation to change. Substance abusers and codependents alike are repeatedly called on in Twelve Step fellowships to have faith and hope. This is the essence of the Second Step: *Came to believe that a Power greater than ourselves could restore us to sanity.*
- *Fellowship:* The fellowships of Al-Anon and Nar-Anon provide strong and constant sources of comfort, advice, and support to loved ones, as well as a vehicle for personal healing and growth through their Twelve Steps and Twelve Traditions.[14]
- *Detaching:* A common wisdom within Twelve Step fellowships goes like this: "Addicts are sick people, not bad people." The underlying belief expressed here is that addicts typically do not get better by being criticized, punished, or rejected. At the same time that the codependent needs to refrain from condemning the substance abuser, she or he must also take concrete steps to stop acting in ways that have

the unintended effect of allowing the substance abuser to remain in denial regarding the truth of his or her problem.[15]

- *Caring detachment* is consistent with the attitude toward addiction and recovery advocated by AA and NA, which states: "We are not responsible for our disease, but we are responsible for our recovery."[16]

The guiding principles behind Al-Anon and Nar-Anon were set forth initially in chapter 8 of *Alcoholics Anonymous.*[17] Written by the wife of a recovering alcoholic, it advocates an approach to dealing with the problem drinker that is reflected in the subsequent publications of Al-Anon and Nar-Anon. This includes admonishing codependents to abandon their efforts to change or shield the alcoholic or addict and to turn their attention instead toward their own spiritual, mental, physical, and social well-being.

The frustration of partners of alcoholics is captured poignantly in the following excerpt from chapter 8: "As animals on a treadmill, we have patiently and wearily climbed, falling back in exhaustion after each futile effort to reach solid ground."[18]

By conceptualizing alcoholism as compulsive behavior that has defied all efforts at self-control, chapter 8 suggests that the only "sane" course of action for the codependent is to "let go," to stop protecting the substance abuser: "We never, never try to arrange a man's life so as to shield him from temptation."[19]

It is apparent how shielding a person from temptation can be dysfunctional. First, it tends to make the codependent, as opposed to the substance abuser, responsible for getting the substance abuser clean and sober. Although some behavioral models of working with significant others do seek to intervene directly on this level,[20] by and large this is not the approach advocated within Twelve Step fellowships. For one thing, these fellowships assume that loved ones have already tried—numerous times and unsuccessfully—to get the alcoholic or addict to stop the addictive behavior.

A second reason not to shield someone from the temptation to use is that this can easily lead to shielding the addict from the negative consequences of use. If AA suggests a way for loved ones to effectively motivate problem drinkers to change, that way could be described as indirect. Consider the following advice from *Alcoholics Anonymous*:

- "... lay the groundwork for a friendly talk about his alcoholic problem.... Be sure you are not critical during such a discussion."[21]
- "Wait until repeated stumbling convinces him he must act, for the more you hurry him the longer his recovery may be delayed."[22]
- "... after his next binge, ask him if he would really like to get over drinking for good. Do not ask that he do it for you or anyone else. Just would he *like* to?"[23]

Such advice is more consistent with subtly encouraging motivation for change through what Al-Anon calls "caring detachment" than it is with attempting to shape behavioral change through reward or punishment. Both philosophically and practically, AA and Al-Anon are much more compatible with the former than the latter approach.

AA and Al-Anon consistently advise loved ones to resist any temptation to shield the problem drinker or user from the natural consequences of drinking or drug use. Here is an example of the advice AA offers in this regard:

> Frequently, you have felt obliged to tell your husband's employer and his friends that he was sick, when as a matter of fact he was tight. Avoid answering these inquiries as much as you can. Whenever possible, let your husband explain.[24]

The last reason is that Al-Anon and Nar-Anon, like AA, are strong proponents of spiritual renewal and character growth. In fact, some newcomers to Al-Anon or Nar-Anon may be initially dismayed by the *lack* of talk about alcoholics and addicts at some meetings. These meetings may simply have evolved to the point where the emphasis is decidedly on the growth and well-being of the members, as opposed to the status of their drinking or using partners, who are left to be responsible for themselves. As one veteran Al-Anon member, whose husband had been in recovery for twenty years, put it:

> I've always been a real controller. Al-Anon helped me learn how to let others be responsible for themselves. I really think that Al-Anon saved my life, because I was drained, spiritually and physically, from always trying to be in control. That's why I still go to meetings regularly—not because my husband drinks, because he doesn't, but just for me.

Al-Anon, Nar-Anon, and Family Therapy

Family therapy has evolved into a clinical specialty within the mental health professions. Different schools of family therapy view the causes of dysfunction differently; consequently, their approaches to intervention differ. It is important to understand that none of the Twelve Step fellowships, including Al-Anon and Nar-Anon, which are the main focus here, have any formal connection with family therapy as a discipline. Although one can superimpose a psychological "theory" on how they work, Twelve Step fellowships espouse no such theories themselves. Rather, they exist and have evolved as mutual-help groups, remaining intentionally nonprofessional.[25]

All Twelve Step fellowships are based on the assumption that addiction is a *primary* dysfunction or diagnosis. In other words, they do not regard substance abuse and addiction as symptoms of some other family dysfunction or individual problem. Accordingly, the emphasis in Twelve Step meetings, whether AA or Al-Anon, is on addiction and even more specifically, on individual recovery from addiction, much more so than on any other issue. This means that staying sober will always be the main focus in AA and Al-Anon (although the latter interprets "sobriety" as that term applies to codependents). Once sober, the individual member of a Twelve Step fellowship is invited to pursue a program of spiritual renewal and character development by "working" the Twelve Steps in his or her day-to-day life.

Al-Anon and Nar-Anon do not regard substance abuse or addiction as symptoms of family dysfunction or personal psychopathology, in the sense that family dysfunction or psychopathology could be said to be *etiological* of substance abuse. On the contrary, they are much more inclined to regard substance abuse and addiction as etiological of other family dysfunctions, including marital conflict, spousal abuse, poor boundaries, childhood depression, and adolescent alienation. Moreover, once the recovery process has begun (but not before then), members of Twelve Step fellowships are apt to have faith that many of these other family problems may be able to be successfully resolved.

This perspective on substance abuse, addiction, and its sequelae can be uncomfortable to family therapists who have been trained to detect family dysfunction and to regard it as etiological of addiction. In a sense, the Twelve Step view challenges family therapists to let go of whatever preconceived notions of etiology they may have learned and to view families and family dysfunction through a different lens—in effect, to entertain the reverse hypothesis. Family therapists wishing to explore this route to family healing are invited to try the FRP methods described in this book. To do so successfully, however, they must be open to the idea that addiction is the *cause* of spiraling family dysfunction, not a result of it, and also that this spiral can begin to be reversed when even one significant other starts relating to the addicted family member through caring detachment.

From the point of view of Al-Anon and Nar-Anon, then, family recovery is a process that begins when one or more members of a family that has been affected by addiction begin the process of recovery. Specifically, that means taking the First Step, which is to acknowledge that one is powerless over another person's addiction (and consequently, not responsible for it). This begins to move the relationship from an enabling relationship with the substance abuser toward a relationship characterized by caring detachment. As simple as this may sound, it is no small feat. It also has profound implications for the individual, for the substance abuser–codependent relationship, and indeed, for the whole family. Some of these implications are explored in this text.

Goals and Objectives of the Family Recovery Program

The structured Family Recovery Program (FRP) that is described in detail in part 2 of this book has specific goals and objectives. These are described in the discussion to follow. The reader should be aware that this treatment protocol is highly focused. Consequently, the same issues are raised repeatedly, and progress toward achieving goals and objectives is monitored continuously. The same issue (e.g., caring detachment) may be approached many times, each time from a slightly different perspective, in an effort to find one or more such perspectives that the client can relate to.

Experience has taught us that it is very easy for even experienced therapists to drift away from the specific goals of the FRP. At times, it is client resistance that accounts for this drift, because some of the "recovery tasks" clients are asked to do between sessions may arouse discomfort or anxiety. Maximum benefit will be achieved when such drifting is minimized. Accordingly, practitioners are encouraged to review the format for sessions in advance and make every effort to cover all of the material.

Treatment Goal 1: Active Participation in the Al-Anon or Nar-Anon Fellowship

Specific Objectives:

- Attending *meetings*
- Getting and using member phone numbers or e-mail addresses, both in times of crisis and more generally so as to develop a *social network*
- Getting and establishing a relationship with a *sponsor*
- Reading and responding to suggested *readings* from fellowship literature

Treatment Goal 2: Caring Detachment

Specific Objectives:

- Decrease in self-reported enabling behaviors
- *Acceptance:* Self-reported acceptance of personal loss of

control (powerlessness) over the substance abuser's drinking or drug-using behavior and an expressed willingness to turn over the fate of the substance abuser to a Higher Power.

- *Surrender:* An expressed willingness to accept the support and advice of the Al-Anon or Nar-Anon fellowship in one's efforts to resist enabling and to detach, and an expressed faith in some Higher Power.
- Increased interest in and commitment to personal growth and development on the part of the significant other (e.g., making new friends, renewed interest in work or personal health, etc.)

Readings, Handouts, and Journaling

Concerned significant others who participate in this program are asked to read specific parts of the following publications: *Al-Anon Faces Alcoholism* and *Alcoholics Anonymous.*[26] *Note:* Al-Anon Faces Alcoholism *is out of print. Please visit Amazon.com or other used booksellers to purchase a copy. If you are unable to find a copy, you may want to substitute other resources for the reading assignments. Al-Anon/Alateen (http://www.al-anon.alateen.org/english.html) has pamphlets and books available for purchase.* In the case of loved ones of drug users, selected readings from *Narcotics Anonymous* may be substituted.[27] Selected pamphlets are also included as reading assignments.

Handouts that link to the eight core topics described below and in more detail in part 2 are provided on an accompanying CD-ROM. In addition to highlighting the reading assignment for each session, the handouts include "homework" or "recovery tasks" or exercises for the client that serve as a review of the material covered for a specific topic and an opportunity to explore this material on a deeper level.

Clients are also asked to maintain journals in which they record their reactions to readings and discussions, as well as their reactions to all Twelve Step meetings they attend. As much as possible, the practitioner should make specific efforts to incorporate journal entries and reactions to readings into the therapeutic dialogue.

Program Overview

The Family Recovery Program (FRP) consists of *eight core topics* plus a *termination* session. These can be delivered through individual counseling sessions or they can be used as topics for a group. Working with groups has the advantage of providing a context in which participants can be encouraged to initially attend meetings together and otherwise network with one another, much the way they are encouraged to network within Al-Anon or Nar-Anon. The FRP treatment protocol typically allows a total of twelve outpatient sessions within a twenty-four-week period. An additional two emergency sessions may be held either within the twenty-four-week treatment period or up to six months following completion of treatment. These sessions, which are initiated by the client, should be reserved for situations in which some significant interaction has occurred between the client and the substance abuser. Other treatment parameters, however, may be used, depending on the treatment milieu. For example, in a concentrated program for significant others of substance abusers, sessions may be held daily.

In the context of the Family Recovery Program, it is the ***significant other*** of the substance abuser who is the client. FRP can be applied to partners, parents, grandparents, and even adult children of substance abusers. It is important, however, that this person (or persons) have frequent contact with the substance abuser. Clinically, we have found that those seeking treatment are, in general, family members or partners on whom the substance abuser is dependent in one way or another.

The eight core topics of the program are as follows:

Topic 1: Introduction and Assessment
Topic 2: The Principles of Twelve Step Fellowships
Topic 3: Al-Anon and Nar-Anon
Topic 4: Denial
Topic 5: Enabling
Topic 6: Acceptance
Topic 7: Caring Detachment
Topic 8: Surrender

Session Guidelines and Checklists

Easy-to-use session guidelines and checklists for facilitators are also included on the accompanying CD-ROM. These guidelines can be printed and used as a reference tool when conducting actual treatment sessions with an individual client or group. The guidelines highlight the important aspects of each core topic that should be covered in each session and provide a way for facilitators to simply check off whether these items were, indeed, discussed—allowing busy therapists to better track what "unfinished business" may still have to be covered in upcoming sessions.

Chapter 2 || Al-Anon, Nar-Anon, and Family Recovery

Family Recovery Program

The overall goal of the Family Recovery Program (FRP) is to help significant others of substance abusers alter their relationship with the substance abuser in such a way as to move from *enabling* toward *caring detachment*. As part of this process, the therapist seeks to facilitate the gradual involvement of the significant other in a Twelve Step fellowship such as Al-Anon or Nar-Anon. *Note: The term* therapist *is meant to include all professionals who work in the area of addiction and recovery, such as experienced clinicians and those who are training to be clinical social workers, clinical psychologists, family therapists, and substance abuse counselors.* The therapist also educates the significant other about the nature of addiction and recovery, and how enabling has the unintended effect or promoting addiction. Finally, the therapist explains the basic principles and "rules of the road" of fellowships such as Al-Ann and Nar-Anon. The role of the therapist, as well as the structure of treatment, is described in this chapter.

The FRP can be thought of as "unilateral family therapy" in the sense that it seeks to alter relational (and even family) dynamics by facilitating change in even a single family member. In other words, the FRP therapist believes that by helping significant others change, the stage is set for the substance abuser to also change.

In this treatment model, the primary agent of change is thought to be a Twelve Step fellowship (Al-Anon or Nar-Anon). Although the therapist can be a vital source of support, advice, and information, the therapist must also make sure that the client understands the importance of "getting active" in Al-Anon or Nar-Anon for the simple reason that, while therapy is time-limited, the support that can be found through fellowship is not. Through involvement in one of these fellowships, the loved one of a substance abuser can receive ongoing advice, comfort, and support. This perspective on the "agent of change" is not meant to diminish in any way the importance of the therapeutic relationship or to minimize the skills needed by the practitioner to successfully implement this program; rather, the intention is to keep the focus clear as to the primary responsibility of the professional and what will be gained when a client successfully bonds to Al-Anon or Nar-Anon.

Role of the FRP Therapist

The therapist who follows the Family Recovery Program seeks to establish a *collaborative* relationship with the client. By approaching treatment as a collaborative venture, the therapist communicates confidence in the significant other—confidence that with some guidance and support, the significant other can successfully alter the nature of his or her relationship with the substance abuser. The FRP therapist is knowledgeable regarding the principles of Twelve Step recovery and is, therefore, in a position to educate the client with respect to Twelve Step recovery. The FRP therapist also uses his or her knowledge regarding the nature of recovery to confront the client in a respectful way regarding behavior and attitudes that may unwittingly promote addiction while simultaneously undermining the significant other's own mental and physical health.

Specific descriptions of the role of the FRP therapist follow:

Education and Advocacy

The therapist acts as a resource and advocate of the Twelve Step approach to recovery in the following ways:

- Explains the AA and NA view of alcoholism or addiction as a chronic progressive disorder marked by loss of control and negative consequences associated with substance use (i.e., "unmanageability").
- Helps the client assess the extent to which alcohol or other drug use (or both) has made the substance abuser's life progressively more unmanageable.
- Helps the client assess the extent to which the substance abuser's drinking or other drug use has made his or her own life progressively more unmanageable.

- Identifies "denial" as it is reflected in the substance abuser's attitudes toward drinking or using drugs, as well as in the significant other's attitudes toward the substance abuser's behavior. *Denial is viewed here as a symbiotic process in which the substance abuser and the significant other each play a role in shielding the* substance abuser *from the natural consequences of substance abuse, refusing to admit or minimizing those consequences, or both.*
- Introduces several key Twelve Step concepts and helps the client understand them by identifying specific experiences that illustrate them.
- Introduces, explains, and advocates reliance on the fellowships of AA or NA for the problem drinker and Al-Anon or Nar-Anon for the significant other.
- Explains how to make use of various Al-Anon or Nar-Anon resources.
- Defines *recovery* as an ongoing process of *arrest* of addiction, as opposed to a so-called *cure.*
- Explains the role of a sponsor and helps the client identify what to look for in choosing an initial Al-Anon or Nar-Anon sponsor.
- Answers questions to the best of his or her ability about material found in AA or NA and Al-Anon or Nar-Anon literature.

Guidance and Advice

The therapist actively and systematically encourages the significant other's involvement in Al-Anon or Nar-Anon in the following ways:

- Monitors the significant other's ongoing involvement in Al-Anon or Nar-Anon and encourages a progression toward greater involvement and bonding, for example, by the following:

- ▷ Suggesting meetings that require increasing personal involvement, such as Step meetings and closed meetings (as opposed to open discussion meetings)
- ▷ Encouraging the client to volunteer for basic service work, such as making coffee and either setting up for or cleaning up after meetings
- ▷ Encouraging the client to get phone numbers or e-mail addresses and to make contact with Al-Anon or Nar-Anon friends between meetings

- ▶ Assists the client in locating meetings and providing appropriate support for getting codependents to attend and participate. This can include the following:
    - ▷ Problem-solving around issues such as transportation or child care
    - ▷ Role-playing how to ask for phone numbers or e-mail addresses, how to volunteer for responsibilities, how to approach a potential sponsor, and so forth
    - ▷ Role-playing around situations over which the client may express anxiety (e.g., disclosing his or her Al-Anon involvement to the substance abuser)
    - ▷ Arranging for an active Al-Anon or Nar-Anon volunteer to meet the client and escort him or her to one or two initial meetings
    - ▷ Clarifying the role of an Al-Anon or Nar-Anon sponsor, encouraging and assisting the significant other in finding a sponsor
    - ▷ Suggesting recovery tasks that will enhance the significant other's successful integration into the fellowship of Al-Anon or Nar-Anon

Motivation and Support

The therapist makes specific efforts to empathize with the significant other and motivate him or her to use Al-Anon or Nar-Anon in the following ways:

- Demonstrates an empathic understanding of the client's feelings of shame, anger, anxiety, and guilt regarding substance abuse and the unmanageability it has caused: *"I know that it's been hard for you to admit that your spouse is addicted. It brings up a lot of unpleasant emotions."*
- Empathizes with the client's resistance to accept loss of control over addiction and the need to detach from the substance abuser: *"I hear you—you've done everything you can think of to get him (her) to stop. But it's out of your control."*
- Consistently points out the impact of the significant other's behavior on the substance abuser: *"Your spouse sure took notice when you said you had already spent the money you had budgeted for liquor and didn't have any more."*

TREATMENT NOTE

Reinforcing Change in Codependents

The therapist can have a major impact on the significant other's motivation to change the basic dynamics of the substance abuser-codependent relationship. One way to do this (as mentioned earlier) is to be alert for and point out the impact that the significant other's behavior has on the substance abuser. The dynamics of the substance abuser-codependent relationship are usually obvious: The more the codependent stays the same—in other words, the more the substance abuser-codependent relationship remains status quo—the less the substance abuser is inclined to change. At the same time, the significant other's mental and physical health is apt to decline. Clinical experience teaches us time and time again that even relatively small changes in a significant other's behavior can disrupt the status quo and cause reactions in the substance abuser. An action as simple as letting the substance abuser know the significant other is attending Al-Anon, is reading about addiction, or is participating in the FRP, almost always causes the substance abuser to react. Not infrequently, drinking or using decreases, at least temporarily. Most often the substance abuser will become defensive. This is a sure sign that a change in the relationship has been perceived, and the therapist should point that out as well. Sometimes, the couple will even begin a dialogue about substance abuse, unmanageability, and recovery. By pointing out such effects when they become apparent, the therapist counters feelings of hopelessness, empowers the significant other, and encourages change in both partners.

Desired Therapist Characteristics

This section describes the knowledge base and some of the characteristics that may contribute to therapeutic effectiveness when using the FRP. To the extent that a professional possesses or is able to develop these characteristics and knowledge base, she or he may be more effective in using this program.

Therapists Should Have Knowledge of the Recovery Culture

The FRP therapist seeks to promote active participation in Al-Anon or Nar-Anon, to help clients understand key recovery concepts, and to guide clients in their first steps toward caring detachment. To pursue these goals effectively, the therapist does not necessarily need to be either a codependent or a recovering substance abuser. On the other hand, she or he does need to be reasonably knowledgeable of and comfortable with the principles that guide Twelve Step fellowships. These are described in the Steps and Traditions of those fellowships.

To be maximally effective, the therapist should also be familiar with the Al-Anon or Nar-Anon and AA and NA culture as it is reflected in actual meetings. For these reasons, it is important that any professional who is not personally involved in AA or NA or in Al-Anon or Nar-Anon, but who is planning to use this manual-guided FRP approach, attend several open discussion meetings prior to using this manual with a client.

In addition, to be effective as a therapist, the professional using the FRP is encouraged to develop a network of Al-Anon or Nar-Anon contacts: men and women who are active in the fellowship of Al-Anon or Nar-Anon and who could be called on to meet a shy or ambivalent client at a first meeting, to provide the therapist with information about particular meetings, to talk with a client over the phone, and so on. Therapists can develop working relationships with these people by going to meetings on some regular basis or simply by networking with recovering persons they know.

TREATMENT NOTE

The Use of Slogans

Slogans are an integral part of the Twelve Step recovery culture. The therapist should be familiar with at least some of these slogans and should introduce them as they are appropriate in the FRP treatment. These slogans—"Easy does it," "One day at a time," "Let go and let God," "First things first," and so forth—should never be dismissed as mere clichés. Rather, they represent succinct statements of wisdom that are firmly rooted in many recovering persons' real-life experiences. The book *Al-Anon Faces Alcoholism* includes a section that discusses slogans and their meanings.[1]

Therapists Should Be Active, Supportive, and Involved

Therapists should work toward being active, engaging, empathic, and respectfully (i.e., nonjudgmentally) "confrontational" during sessions (as opposed, for example, to being merely reflective, detached, or overly interpretive). Twelve Step–oriented treatment for substance abuse is sometimes stereotyped as an exceedingly confrontational approach whose goal is to "break down" clients' denial; in other words, to confront them until they admit to the problem.[2] The program presented here is *not* an aggressively confrontational therapy. On the contrary, overly aggressive confrontation can come across as accusatory and actually undermine the significant other's motivation. The FRP therapist is a source of information and may be quite frank in sharing perceptions, for example, regarding denial or enabling on the part of the significant other. But the therapist does not lecture or scold clients for their so-called "dysfunctional" attitudes or behavior, much less aggressively challenge their denial. *An effective therapist endeavors to establish a collaborative, supportive, and honest relationship with the client.* As part of this relationship, the therapist may at times be frank, respectfully sharing an observation even if that observation makes the client uncomfortable. But this is true of any good psychotherapy.

Overall, the goal of the therapist is to help the significant other understand and identify denial (i.e., resistance to acceptance) and codependence (i.e., resistance to detaching) as these are revealed in the significant other's decisions, words, and actions in relation to the substance abuser. The therapist confronts the client consistently in a frank but respectful manner regarding attitudes or behaviors that support drinking or drugging or that reflect a lack of understanding of alcoholism or drug addiction, consistently encourages the client to get involved in the fellowships of Al-Anon or Nar-Anon, and helps the client to understand key Al-Anon or Nar-Anon concepts in terms of his or her experiences with the substance abuser.

Therapists should appreciate the fact that Twelve Step concepts allow much room for individual interpretation. Significant others can and should be expected to interpret Twelve Step concepts in light of their own experiences. What may represent an unmanageable life for one person, for example, may not seem quite so unmanageable when viewed through the eyes of another. What is one person's Higher Power may not be another's. And so on. This pluralism is consistent with Twelve Step fellowship traditions, which not only allow but also actively encourage individuality of interpretation within broad guidelines. What is most important is not whether two clients each interpret Twelve Step concepts in precisely the same way; what counts is the end result: acceptance of progressive unmanageability caused by substance abuse and movement toward caring detachment in relation to the substance abuser.

Therapists Provide Focused Treatment

The Family Recovery Program (FRP) seeks to initiate a process that will lead to significant change in a loved one and his or her relationship to a substance abuser, yet it also seeks to accomplish this within a relatively short period of time. *Note: The program presented in part 2 was designed to be implemented in a total of twelve sessions over a period of up to six months. In a case-management environment, practitioners may be pressed to work with an even more modest allocation of services. Under these circumstances, the issue of therapeutic focus becomes paramount.* The program is consequently highly structured and tightly focused. For each client, it becomes a therapeutic challenge to cover as much ground as possible, given the circumstances of the particular case. In general, it is expected that all eight topics can be covered in twelve to fourteen sessions. To be able to accomplish this, the therapist needs to be able and willing to focus treatment and to stay on task. Typically, sessions are scheduled weekly, at least initially, partly to establish rapport and partly to initiate involvement in Al-Anon or Nar-Anon. Later on, meeting every other week may be appropriate, because it allows more time for attending meetings and other opportunities to bond with the fellowship as opposed to the therapist.

At the beginning of each session, through the process of reviewing the previous week, issues relevant to the significant other's life can be expected to come up. The client needs to be given time to articulate his or her problems and concerns and to feel heard by the therapist. At the same time, it's important to keep in mind that the structured nature of this program does not allow therapists to "follow the client" entirely—in other words, to pursue a client's agenda to the exclusion of the FRP's content or objectives. In light of this, it is the therapist's responsibility to keep sessions focused and to avoid getting into lengthy discussions of other matters (job problems, parenting problems, marital problems, etc.). At such times, the therapist is advised to invoke the "first things first" principle: emphasize the client's need to first use the resources of Al-Anon or Nar-Anon, to work on successfully detaching from the substance abuser as a first step toward personal and family recovery, and to defer dealing with other issues until some progress has been made in these areas.

As pointed out earlier, detaching, even in small ways, has clear effects on substance abusers and on relationships. This may lead to beneficial spillover effects in areas about which the client may express concern. Some problems, in fact, may resolve more or less spontaneously once the client has altered the substance abuser–codependent relationship by placing his or her own enabling behaviors and attitudes in check. Other problems may persist and require further attention later on. However, except for instances of active spousal or child abuse or of severe depression with suicidal ideation, loss of social functioning, or both, most collateral issues can usually be put on hold while the client focuses first on learning to detach and, second, on beginning to bond with Al-Anon or Nar-Anon.

The therapist needs to give the client two messages consistently and repeatedly. The first is that enabling invariably reduces the substance abuser's motivation for change, whereas caring detachment can promote motivation for change. Second, successful detaching affects the substance abuser–codependent relationship in ways that will ultimately prove healthier for both the substance abuser and the codependent. Once the change process—from enabling to detaching as the primary way of relating to the substance abuser—is established, collateral issues, such as strained marriages and alienated family relations, may be more effectively addressed, perhaps by adding traditional family or marital therapy into the comprehensive treatment plan. Attempting to address them prior to this, however, may not prove fruitful.

For the addict or alcoholic, the first and foremost goal in early recovery is to get active in AA or NA. "Don't drink, and go to meetings" is the advice invariably given to the newcomer. Similarly, significant others can be advised: *"Don't enable, and go to meetings."* This marks the starting point of not only the recovery for the significant other but also of change in the substance abuser–codependent relationship and in the family.

TREATMENT NOTE:

Avoiding Distractions

Despite the therapist's best efforts, some clients may persist in trying to bring the focus of sessions onto some other issue that they regard as more pressing than the one the therapist wants to discuss. This may reflect denial (of the unmanageability caused by addiction) on the part of the client; alternatively, it may simply reflect an honest difference of opinion about what is more important. Significant others of substance abusers frequently feel overwhelmed as addiction progressively makes life more stressful for everyone. It is understandable under these circumstances that the significant other, on entering the FRP, may have a lengthy "agenda" of concerns. One appropriate response to a client's efforts to divert therapy, for example to discussions about relationship conflicts, work, or other family problems, is to offer assurance that she or he will be referred to an appropriate resource following completion of the FRP should those issues continue to be of concern at that time. In an extreme case, it may be necessary to make a referral so that the client can pursue his or her concern at the same time that he or she participates in the FRP. This would be the case, for example, if there was a clear risk of spousal or child abuse or if the client appears to be clinically depressed.

Although treatment of spousal or child abuse or neglect is not the subject of this book, any professional planning to treat either substance abusers or their significant others needs to be aware of the significant rates of co-occurrence of abuse and addiction. Possible abuse should be explicitly ruled out or dealt with early in treatment. The clinician using the program described here may still proceed so long as any issues of abuse have been identified and triaged to appropriate treatment resources.

Therapists Encourage a Reliance on Al-Anon or Nar-Anon

In this program, it is bonding with the fellowship of Al-Anon or Nar-Anon, and not the therapist-client relationship, that is seen as the primary agent of change. The effective therapist recognizes that active involvement in Al-Anon or Nar-Anon, including regular attendance at a variety of meetings, using the telephone or e-mail to connect with other Al-Anon or Nar-Anon members on a regular basis, reading Al-Anon or Nar-Anon literature, and developing a relationship with a sponsor, is clearly preferable to increasing reliance on the therapist. Similarly, the client should be encouraged to rely on the resources of Al-Anon or Nar-Anon, more so than on the therapist, in times of crisis. Through these efforts, the therapist plays a crucial role in helping to direct the client and get the process of change started.

TREATMENT NOTE

Responding to Crises

The therapist's first response to a client's crisis, aside from sympathy and support, should be to encourage him or her to contact an Al-Anon or Nar-Anon friend or sponsor or to go to a meeting as soon as possible. If the therapist sees the need to schedule an emergency session to deal with a crisis, the goals for such a session should be the following:

- To help the client assess the nature of the crisis in terms of how it threatens his or her personal well-being
- To establish priorities: What can the client do immediately to deal with the problem in a way that is caring but consistent with detaching as opposed to enabling?
- To clarify what resources within Al-Anon or Nar-Anon the client could turn to (calling another member, calling a sponsor, etc.) to support him or her at this time

Session Format

To allow the therapist to cover a fair amount of material in relatively few sessions, the format of FRP therapy sessions is fairly structured in this program. Although the initial (assessment) session and the termination session of this program follow unique formats that are described in detail later, the practitioner should use the following format for all other sessions:

Task 1: Review

Beginning with session 2, each session should start with the therapist checking in with the client by conducting a brief review (approximately ten to fifteen minutes) of the client's experiences since the last session (with special emphasis on Al-Anon or Nar-Anon meetings attended and on the client's efforts to detach in a constructive way from the substance abuser). Detachment efforts include attempts to stop enabling *plus* efforts on the part of the client to take care of his or her personal welfare independent of the substance abuser. This opening portion of each session is crucial to establishing rapport and keeping the agenda of the FRP in focus. As much as possible, the therapist should avoid protracted discussions of collateral issues (work, other family problems, children, etc.). The therapist should keep the focus as much as possible on Al-Anon or Nar-Anon involvement, on the client's efforts to improve his or her own emotional and physical health, and on following up on any recovery tasks that were agreed to at the end of the previous session. (The printable guidelines for each session that are contained on the accompanying CD-ROM can help the therapist maintain this focused approach.) Concrete efforts to detach should be reinforced, and any "slips" the client may have had (i.e., instances of enabling) need to be discussed. In addition to the client's self-report, journal entries and written responses to various handouts can be very helpful in facilitating the review process, in evaluating ongoing progress, and in establishing future recovery tasks.

TREATMENT NOTE

"Slips"

Within AA and NA, a "slip" refers to a time when the alcoholic or addict drinks or uses other drugs. These fellowships traditionally approach such episodes as serious but not altogether unexpected occurrences—hence the commonly used phrase "We seek progress, not perfection."[3] The stated goal of both AA and NA, of course, is abstinence, but they recognize this as a long-term goal that is not typically achieved without setbacks. Even those with many years of sobriety may have occasional slips. What is most important at such times is that the addict or alcoholic be able to go to a meeting for support and disclose the slip. Slips are discussed in a nonjudgmental manner, with the emphasis being on what to do next (i.e., *how to avoid taking the next drink or ingesting the next drug*). The substance abuser who discloses a slip at a meeting can expect to have it acknowledged but without fear of recrimination. Slips are thought of as times when the "powerful, baffling, and cunning" illness of alcoholism or drug addiction has overcome the substance abuser's best intentions to stay clean and sober.[4] "Getting back on the wagon" is what is needed first and foremost at such times, and the group rightly recognizes and reinforces every hour of sobriety following a slip.

Within the context of Al-Anon and Nar-Anon, slips are occasions when a significant other *enables* the substance abuser: either providing the means to drink or use other drugs or else helping the substance abuser avoid or minimize some negative consequence of drinking or other drug use. A slip could also be thought of as a time when a significant other fails to maintain, in words and actions, an attitude of caring detachment toward the substance abuser and, instead, enables addiction, for example by any of these actions:

- *Monitoring* closely the substance abuser's drinking or other drug use. This typically only causes stress in the significant other while not motivating the substance abuser to change. In fact, the substance abuser may use more in response to this.
- Attempting to *hide* or *destroy* liquor or other drugs. This can ignite intense anger and conflict, again stressing the significant other to no benefit.
- *Bargaining* with the substance abuser about how much the person can drink or use drugs. This tends to replicate the substance abuser's own internal battle to "control" his or her addiction.
- *Giving the substance abuser money* under false pretenses: for example, giving the alcoholic "gas money" that everyone knows will be spent on liquor.
- *Covering up* for the substance abuser to an employer, friends, and so on.

The goal of this intervention is to facilitate caring detachment and personal growth within the loved ones of substance abusers. To accomplish this, an open and honest relationship with the therapist is critical. This includes being open about slips, as described earlier. Through such open discussion, clients will develop a better understanding of caring detachment, as well as tolerant attitudes toward themselves as they come to appreciate that detachment is a goal typically achieved incrementally. When discussing slips with clients, the therapist aims to help them decide what to do next (i.e., the best thing to do *after* a slip that is consistent with Al-Anon or Nar-Anon philosophy).

Detaching, much like sobriety, is best thought of as a process characterized by progress that is punctuated by intermittent slips. Initially, significant others can be encouraged to detach in small ways—for instance, by letting the substance abuser know they have chosen to seek help or have started going to Al-Anon or Nar-Anon meetings. Such simple acts break through the conspiracy of avoidance that is critical to enabling addiction to continue. As simple as these acts may sound, however, they often require real courage on the part of the significant other. They can elicit strong reactions in substance abusers for they herald the beginning of change in the substance abuser–codependent relationship.

In addition to briefly reviewing any slips that may have occurred since the last session, some of the review time should be used to talk at least briefly about the client's reactions to readings and to any Al-Anon or Nar-Anon meetings she or he attended since the last session. If no meetings were attended or if the client seems to be resisting going to meetings, the reasons for this resistance should be explored.

Task 2: New Material

Following the review, each session should move on to cover a specific focus: one of the eight core topics of the program as described in part 2. It is very important that the therapist help the client understand all key concepts that are presented in these sessions, not only in an abstract intellectual sense but also concretely, in light of the client's experiences in a relationship with the substance abuser. In other words, the goal of presenting new material is to have it come alive for the client through discussions and examples that draw on the client's interactions with the substance abuser. The therapist needs to be able to point to a specific incident and say, "That is enabling" or "That is what we mean when we talk about detaching."

Task 3: Recovery Tasks

Each session ends with specific suggestions—*recovery tasks*—that clients are asked to follow through on between sessions. These are arrived at collaboratively with the client. Each topic covered in part 2, however, includes many specific suggestions for relevant recovery tasks. Though brief, this last part of the session is very important and should be attended to with care, because recovery tasks are essentially grist for the mill for subsequent sessions.

The therapist should attempt to assign recovery tasks in each of the following areas:

- Meetings: A mutually agreed-on list of Al-Anon or Nar-Anon meetings that are to be attended by the client before the next session.
- Readings: Suggested readings describe or illustrate Twelve Step recovery principles.
- Handouts: Handouts that link to the eight core topics are provided on an accompanying CD-ROM. In addition to highlighting the reading assignment for each session, the handouts include "homework" exercises for the client that serve as a review of the material and an opportunity to explore this material on a deeper level.
- Fellowship involvement: Suggested activities will help to facilitate the client's active involvement and bonding with Al-Anon or Nar-Anon, such as making contact with Al-Anon or Nar-Anon members, approaching a potential sponsor, and so forth.

- Caring detachment: Suggestions will explain specific things the client can do to decrease his or her enabling of the substance abuser and increase caring detachment.

Chapter 3 || On Giving Advice

Therapist and Client Interaction

The issue of how significant others can best deal with a loved one who is an addict or alcoholic is, of course, the focus of this book and the Family Recovery Program (FRP). Most, if not all, significant others will have made the decision to seek counseling at least in part, not for themselves, but to get concrete advice on how to get their loved ones to stop substance use, how to get them into treatment, or what to do when their loved one gets drunk or in trouble. These are all reasonable and common concerns. They are usually the results of chronic frustration and feelings of defeat. Not infrequently, significant others will have tried, unsuccessfully, for years to accomplish these very goals.

In responding to clients, and particularly when asked for specific advice about what to do, the therapist needs to be sure that whatever advice is given is consistent with Twelve Step fellowship traditions and philosophies. When offering advice, it is important to keep in mind that AA, Al-Anon, and other Twelve Step fellowships are remarkably pluralistic and nondogmatic. They have a spiritual core, and they possess a fund of wisdom about addiction and recovery. Aside from their singular emphasis on abstinence as the goal of recovery, however, they are remarkably flexible: spiritually pluralistic and decidedly pragmatic about how to stay sober one day at a time. They implicitly recognize that the useful strategies for staying clean and sober (or its equivalent in significant others, which is maintaining an attitude of caring detachment in word and deed) are as varied as the number of people who make up the fellowships. The bottom line is what works for the individual substance abuser or his or her loved one (how successful she or he is in staying clean and sober or in detaching). Although it is true that Twelve Step fellowships use slogans heavily, these reflect broad statements of philosophy, not specific advice. Therapists should adopt a similarly flexible and pragmatic approach when offering advice.

Al-Anon and Nar-Anon traditions suggest that it is best to approach the issue of advice giving in a collaborative way—

as something that is flexible and, therefore, open to discussion—as opposed to presenting it in any way as dogma handed down by the therapist. The understated subtitle of a popular AA publication, *Living Sober*,[1] for example, is simply this: "Some methods A.A. members have used for not drinking." Similarly, recovery tasks and suggestions about detachment strategies are best approached as practical suggestions, which clients are free to modify to suit their particular situations and their relationships to the substance abusers. For example, strategies that would make sense for a spouse to use might have to be modified for a parent, sibling, or adult child of a substance abuser.

The therapist should also be aware that what works for one significant other may be precisely the wrong thing for another. Consider the following example:

> The wife of an alcoholic man was accustomed to confronting him and complaining often about his drinking. Over a period of years, this dynamic had come to represent the status quo for the relationship. The alcoholic had grown accustomed to it. He knew that at least once a week, he and his wife would argue about his drinking. But he also knew that that would be the end of it. The storm would pass, and the next day everything would be back to "normal" in the house. In an ironic way, the fighting served to enable his drinking, because it was a sign that nothing in the relationship had changed. So they kept on fighting, and he kept on drinking.

For another spouse, the situation was exactly the opposite. This relationship had evolved into a conspiracy of silence about drinking. The wife never mentioned it, although both spouses knew very well that she was concerned about his behavior. She just avoided her husband when he was drunk, and she never brought up the issue when he was sober. In this case, it was silence, not fighting, that represented the enabling response. Silence between this couple represented the relational status quo. So long as the wife was silent, the husband, like the one in the first example, could feel secure that nothing had really changed and he could go on drinking as usual.

In guiding each of these wives toward caring detachment, the same therapist offered them exactly the opposite advice. To the first, she advised *not* fighting. Instead, she suggested leaving the house to spend time with other family or friends or to go to an Al-Anon meeting whenever her husband got drunk. In contrast, she advised the second wife to start to comment to her husband—when he was *sober*—on how much he drank and how much money he spent every week on liquor. The therapist cautioned this wife not to get into a shouting match with her husband when he was drinking or to debate whether he was an alcoholic. She was told to simply remark about the amount, the frequency, and the cost.

These examples on giving advice illustrate the fact that concepts such as enabling and detaching reflect *dynamic processes* within the substance abuser–codependent relationship. Contrary to what some therapists may expect, there are few hard and fast rules as to which behaviors constitute enabling and which constitute detaching. Obviously, stopping at a liquor store every day on the way home from work and buying your alcoholic spouse a fifth of vodka would constitute enabling, period. And allowing a substance abuser to experience the negative consequences of drinking or drug use without any effort on your part to mitigate those consequences would certainly constitute detaching. Many other situations, however, are less clear. Determining what is enabling and what is caring detachment depends, in part, on understanding the dynamics of the relationship and then deciding what behavior would represent a change in the status quo—in other words, what would help the codependent break old, ineffective patterns of relating and thereby send a message to the substance abuser that something has changed. In both of the examples given, the alcoholics had clear and immediate reactions to the change in their wives' behavior—to the change in the dynamics of their *relationships*. Moreover, both wives reported that the new ways of relating made them feel better about themselves.

Al-Anon and Nar-Anon, as fellowships of individuals who are in relationships with alcoholics or addicts, have strong traditions of providing unqualified support as well as a wealth of practical advice to all who wish to avail themselves of it. Al-Anon and Nar-Anon are widespread, and their resources are readily available. The therapist should attempt to steer the client consistently toward Al-Anon or Nar-Anon as *the* primary source of support and advice about what to do about his or her relationship with the substance abuser. The resources that Al-Anon and Nar-Anon have to offer include meetings, telephone and e-mail networks, hot lines, sponsors, and literature.

As another example of a situation that might arise, consider this scenario:

> A woman has her therapist paged in the middle of the night. She is extremely distressed. Her husband, she says, was just arrested for driving while intoxicated and is in the local lockup. This is his first arrest; nevertheless, she is worried it will mean that her husband will miss more time from work, where he has already been in trouble for excessive absences, and that he will get a poor performance evaluation that could lead to his being laid off. Worse still, she fears that he may be subject to immediate dismissal if it's discovered that he has been arrested or if he is sentenced to jail time. On the one hand, she realizes that this arrest is just another in a long string of negative consequences that are the result of her husband's alcoholism. Part of her wants to detach: to let him face the consequences, rather than mitigating those consequences by going to the lockup and bonding him out. However, she is conflicted over how to respond to her husband's emphatic demand that she drive immediately to the lockup and post bond and also hire an attorney. In a phone conversation with her, he was alternately tearful, angry, pleading, and threatening, saying things like "I can't stand being locked up like an animal" and that "This will destroy us unless we fight it, starting right now."

The therapist may understandably feel pressed to give an immediate response to this woman. Indeed, some therapeutic response is called for. However, this can be done in one of two ways. First, the therapist could help the client work through her ambivalence and reach a decision, right there over the phone. Given the demands of the woman's husband, both the client and the therapist could feel pressured to work the issue through and reach a decision immediately. However, another approach would be to ask the client if she had considered calling or texting an Al-Anon friend, or her sponsor if she has one, or even deferring a decision until she could get to a meeting and talk it out. The therapist in this situation could reinforce the idea that no matter what the client decides to do, she should recognize how difficult her position is and how painful it can be to detach. The therapist can validate that it is appropriate for the client to take some time to think and to take advantage of Al-Anon as a place to vent her thoughts and feelings and to seek comfort and support. The therapist can point out sympathetically that this very situation has no doubt been faced by many others and that knowing what others have done and seeking their counsel and support can be a great stress reliever.

Should the therapist decide to help this client reach a decision, then the therapist should be guided by the general principle of helping the codependent identify alternate courses of action, by deciding which would be enabling and which would be detaching, and by encouraging the detached response as being the better one in the long run. In this example, a first step might be to ask the wife what she would usually do in a similar situation and what would be the likely consequences of that course of action on her husband's drinking in the long run. Another way to put it is this: "If you were to bail your husband out tonight, would that motivate him to think about not drinking or would it help maintain the status quo?"

Al-Anon and Nar-Anon clearly advocate caring detachment and favor allowing the drinker or user to experience the natural consequences of substance use. In this example, that would mean not bailing out the alcoholic husband, at least not immediately. His wife may need a great deal of emotional support for that decision. The therapist must be able to sympathize with the anxieties that detaching creates and support the courage that it takes to break free from enabling. This is no mean task and requires, at times, a virtual leap of faith—a belief in the ultimate wisdom of "tough love." This is what is meant by *surrender* within the Al-Anon and Nar-Anon fellowships. It is also why Al-Anon and Nar-Anon are so important, for they will continue to be there for the client long after treatment has been terminated.

Should the client give in to her anxieties and bail out her husband, the therapist must be careful not to judge her harshly for that decision. Rather, the therapist should recognize that detachment is hard work and suggest that perhaps the client can begin detaching in less stressful situations. Detachment is a process that can be shaped, beginning with small actions and leading to bolder ones. One useful approach to this is to help the significant other develop a *detaching hierarchy* that starts by identifying little ways to detach and then identifies progressively bolder steps toward caring detachment. In this example, not bailing out the husband would clearly fall on the "bolder detaching" side of the hierarchy.

The same resources that are available to the client are also available to the therapist. Specifically, chapter 8 ("To Wives") in *Alcoholics Anonymous*, the stories in *Al-Anon Faces Alcoholism*, and Al-Anon and Nar-Anon meetings are all resources the therapist can turn to for guidance in giving advice to clients.[2] Therapists who are aware of and avail themselves of these materials and resources may have an advantage in counseling clients who are making difficult decisions.

Chapter 4 || Motivating the Substance Abuser to Change

Admitting Powerlessness

Virtually all significant others of substance abusers would like a concrete answer to the question that nags them: What can I do to get my loved one to give up alcohol or other drugs? It has already been suggested here that detaching promotes reevaluation and change in the substance abuser–codependent relationship, whereas enabling undermines any motivation for such reevaluation or change. Paradoxically, Al-Anon and Nar-Anon initiate the change process by asking loved ones to admit they are powerless, by themselves, to change the substance abusers' behavior. *This is Step One: We admitted we were powerless over alcohol—that our lives had become unmanageable.*[1]

Another way of framing this to a client is to suggest that the current dynamics of his or her relationship with the substance abuser effectively promotes the status quo instead of promoting change; in other words, "The way you've been relating to the substance abuser hasn't promoted significant or lasting change, so why not put that aside for a while and try a different approach?"

Significant Others as Agents of Change

Behaviorally oriented family therapies for substance abuse also recognize that problems such as substance abuse can be influenced by social consequences within the family. Therapists using this approach attempt to effect change through behavioral interventions, most often enlisting the spouse as the agent of change.[2] Some such approaches to intervention with concerned significant others, most notably the Community Reinforcement Approach (CRA),[3] advocate shaping the substance abuser's drinking or drug use through the direct application of reward, extinction, or response incompatibility strategies by the loved one. For example, the wife of an alcoholic may be encouraged to praise her husband whenever he does not drink and also to offer other reinforcements, such as physical affection or small gifts. In contrast, she may be encouraged to show no response at all to his continued using or drinking (i.e., extinction).

And she may be encouraged to engage her husband in activities (e.g., going to a movie) that are incompatible with drinking. CRA advises loved ones to avoid excessive arguing with the substance abuser in the belief that punishment is not as effective as reward and extinction in altering behavior.

The goals of behaviorally oriented interventions, such as CRA and this FRP Twelve Step-oriented intervention, overlap to the extent that both see motivating a substance abuser to change as desirable. However, the approaches have significant differences. CRA clearly seeks to use loved ones as primary agents of change by teaching them behavior modification techniques. In CRA, the goal of treatment is primarily motivating the substance abuser to drink or use less, with improving the overall mental health of the significant other being more or less secondary. In contrast, in the FRP, which relies on Al-Anon and Nar-Anon, the emphasis is reversed, with more importance placed on the recovery and growth of the *loved one*. Getting the substance abuser to stop or decrease use or get into treatment is desirable, but it is also seen as being more likely to occur as the loved ones' emotional, spiritual, and physical health improve and as they change how they relate to the substance abuser in a fundamental way.

Caring Detachment

The Twelve Step approach to motivating the substance abuser to change, then, differs from behavioral approaches, such as CRA, in philosophy and approach. The concept of caring detachment emphasizes allowing the substance abuser to experience the natural consequences of his or her problem, as opposed to shielding him or her in any way, and asks significant others to place responsibility for recovery on the substance abusers, while focusing on their own emotional, social, and spiritual needs. This is not to say that the concerned significant other rejects, attacks, or rebukes the substance abuser. However, the result of successful detachment is a vastly different substance abuser–codependent relationship and a much healthier codependent. One mother of two adult alcoholic sons put it this way:

> I realized it was time for me to let them go and for me to take care of me. Even if they died—and this is really difficult for me to say—I knew that I would go on. I had done my best—I had loved them—and now I had to let them go.[4]

Al-Anon describes caring detachment in the following way:

> For Al-Anon members, detachment is the culmination of applying themselves to all the steps and slogans of the Al-Anon program, especially the first step. This necessitates accepting a concept of powerlessness over another human being and over alcoholism. In order to reach the kind of detachment that Al-Anon members strive for, the individual must come to understand and accept his or her own feelings, attitudes, prejudices and actions and be committed to changing them in a healthy way.[5]

Clearly, the foregoing passage suggests that the process of detaching from the substance abuser goes beyond merely allowing him or her to suffer the natural consequences of the problem, unmitigated by concerned others. Such behaviors may be signs of detachment, but detachment itself appears to be a process of significant internal change or growth as well, including developing the capacity for humility and acceptance. These same sentiments are expressed in the following words of Carolyn W., a woman who was the wife of an alcoholic and the mother of four chemically dependent sons:

> Learning to detach is a great kindness to ourselves and to the chemically dependent person, and well worth overcoming the obstacles in the beginning. One reward of detachment is that it frees us to grow, to "live and let live."[6]

The foregoing quote recognizes, again, that the goal of detachment is not achieved easily and requires substantial internal changes in attitudes and beliefs to support its outward behavioral manifestations. Indeed, sustained detachment could be said to be the result of a profound change in a person's outlook on life and on relationships in general. This seems to be the case for those who are seen as models of caring detachment. Carolyn W. goes on to offer the following advice for those who wish to pursue this goal:

> In the process of rebuilding our relationship, I've found several things that help in my emotional and mental stability, and help guide me through detachment:
>
> 1. The absence of suspicion and resentment. Nursing a grudge was a major factor in my unhappiness.
>
> 2. Not living in the past. An unwholesome preoccupation with old mistakes and failures leads to depression.
>
> 3. Not wasting time and energy fighting conditions I cannot change. I cooperate with life instead of trying to run away from it.
>
> 4. I force myself to stay involved with others. I resist the temptation to withdraw and become reclusive during periods of emotional stress.
>
> 5. I refuse to indulge in self-pity when life hands me a raw deal.
>
> 6. I cultivate the old-fashioned virtues—love, honor, compassion, loyalty.[7]

Two things stand out in Carolyn W.'s list. The first is that detachment as a *pattern of behavior* (e.g., not bailing out a partner who has been arrested for the second time for driving while intoxicated) correlates with detachment as a *set of values* and an approach to relationships and to life in general. Although FRP therapists will be asking significant others to identify and try out behaviors consistent with detaching, they should recognize that there is a level deeper than this—a constellation of character traits that underlie and support these new ways of relating to the substance abuser and, indeed, to one's self. The process of character growth and spiritual renewal that leads to this result is best achieved when the individual bonds to a Twelve Step fellowship and begins to incorporate the Twelve Step program in his or her day-to-day life.

Step Twelve of AA explicitly recognizes the profound nature of this change when it talks about spiritual awakening: "Having had a spiritual awakening as the result of these steps, we tried to carry this message to alcoholics, and to practice these principles in all our affairs."[8] This step applies to Al-Anon as well. Often associated in peoples' minds only with becoming a sponsor and "spreading the word" of recovery, the Twelfth Step actually emphasizes the need to live a life consistent with the Steps, most of which have more to do with character development than addiction. This may well explain why a single family member's recovery can, in the long run, affect an entire family so profoundly.

The second noteworthy aspect of Carolyn W.'s list is that there is no inherent incompatibility between detachment and loyalty: One can be loyal yet still detach. In fact, detaching may be more loving than enabling. This detaching is often called *tough love*. The idea of detaching as loyal and loving is an important point to keep in mind, because substance abusers often accuse their loved ones of disloyalty when they first begin to detach.

This discussion of detachment is relevant in several ways to the issue of motivating the substance abuser to change. It is important because although substance abuse and addiction are problems of the individual, they also have a relational component. As we shall see later, addiction itself can be framed in relational terms. In addition, relational patterns between the substance abuser and the codependent can either support the addictive process (enabling) or undermine it (detaching). As emphasized previously, enabling refers to those attitudes and behaviors in the codependent that support the status quo in the relationship, thereby also supporting the addictive process. Conversely, detaching upsets the relational status quo. Time and again, we have seen how successful detaching affects not only the codependent but the substance abuser as well. The therapist should keep this fact in mind, because loved ones not infrequently become anxious when it is suggested that they "let go" of the substance abuser. If uninformed about the true nature and dynamics of detaching, they may mistake such advice for rejecting or giving up on the substance abuser, indeed on the relationship itself. It will be important to assure clients that changing the way they relate to the substance abuser will prove, in the long run, to be the most effective way to motivate him or her to change and is, in truth, an act of caring. The following two examples illustrate this.

Example of Caring Detachment: Margaret

Margaret sought out treatment for herself because she felt depressed and hopeless about her situation. She was sixty years old and a successful administrator in a state agency. Normally, she would have been looking forward to a comfortable retirement, but unfortunately, her situation was anything but normal. She had three grown sons, ranging in age from twenty-six to thirty-four, all of whom lived with her and all of whom were alcoholics. The oldest had been unemployed since losing his driver's license six months earlier, following a third arrest for driving while intoxicated. He was also divorced, and when he had his five-year-old daughter on alternate weekends, he pretty much handed her over to Margaret.

Widowed when her youngest son was three years old, Margaret had supported all of her sons by herself. Their father had also been an alcoholic, though he had managed to work steadily and was not abusive. She described him as "a quiet drunk—basically a sweet man, but with little confidence, who loved me in his way." As the sole parent, she tended to be somewhat indulgent of her sons. "I've never liked saying no to them," she explained. "For a long time, whenever I'd say no, I'd feel guilty—like I had traumatized them. It took me a while to realize that they were just 'normally' frustrated and angry."

Margaret was almost as indulgent now as she had been when her sons were boys. When she sought out treatment (because she was feeling depressed, drained, and hopeless), she was doing virtually all the cooking and cleaning in the house and paid all the major household expenses. Her sons spent their earnings mostly on cars, clothes, and booze. The longest any one of them had lived away from home was six months, when the youngest one did a semester at college before dropping out.

It was understandable that Margaret saw her situation as hopeless. There seemed no end in sight to her sons' dependency—on her and on alcohol. The few times she had broached the subjects with any of them about moving out or doing something about drinking, she'd been rebuffed. Although she recognized her own depression, what she needed most of all, she said, was some guidance in changing her situation. Someone had told her about Al-Anon and the idea of letting go of her sons, but she had not yet been to a meeting, and she had no idea of what "letting go" meant. Despite her frustrations, she still loved her sons. Moreover, on some level, she still felt guilty and responsible for their addictions, for in her words, "I want to help them, not reject them." To her way of thinking, her friend's advice smacked of rejection.

In Margaret's case, it did indeed take some doing for her to see the difference between caring detachment and rejection. As it turned out, this was partly because she did harbor resentments toward her sons—resentments that she had been reluctant to admit. Secretly, she feared that once she allowed herself to express anger, she might explode with rage. When she was able to accept these feelings and find a sympathetic ear in her therapist, she was able to work them through to the extent that she no longer feared that detaching would turn into cruel rejection. She started going to Al-Anon meetings. The first two she went to didn't appeal to her, but her counselor continued to encourage her to attend meetings. They both networked among friends and finally found two meetings in which Margaret felt quite comfortable. Within a month, she had a sponsor whom she spoke with over the phone and via e-mail several times a week and often met for coffee on Sunday mornings.

Margaret started to detach in small ways. This is the approach advocated because it is typically less threatening and leads to initial successes that help to boost the codependent's self-confidence. Margaret began by making a point of meeting friends for dinner or eating at their houses two or three times a week, leaving her sons to fend for themselves when it came to dinner. She also started sorting the laundry piles, doing her own and leaving her sons' for them. The response was immediate. "They're all complaining," she said to her therapist with a laugh, "that there's no food in the house and that they have no clothes to wear!" Margaret responded to these complaints in the way she and her therapist had decided: She told her sons that she thought it was neither in her interest nor theirs to continue to do all the cooking or cleaning. That was treating them like children, she explained, when they were obviously grown men. Grudgingly, they started making their own arrangements for meals several times a week. Margaret noticed that they complained, but they did not starve.

Next, Margaret asked her sons to start contributing $50 a week each toward the household expenses—heat, electricity, and so on. They complained again, all three saying that they couldn't afford it. Her unemployed son accused her of "kicking him when he was down." But Margaret stuck to her guns. She knew very well that her sons seemed able enough to come up with drinking money, but until now, she'd never said anything about it. Now she said this:

> We all have expenses, and we all have to decide how we're going to spend our money. I've been thinking about selling this house anyway, because it's becoming too expensive to maintain on my income alone. I have to start planning for retirement. I've been thinking about doing that in two years. At that point, I plan to sell the place and buy a condominium. But if you men can't help support it until then, I may have to sell it sooner.

Again, the men complained, but somehow they each came up with their $50. Her unemployed son found a job, and one of the others drove him there and back every day. Margaret also noticed that they were using the washer and dryer more often and that the refrigerator had some food in it.

The last thing Margaret did was to leave the materials she'd been reading—about alcoholism—in the living room where her sons could see them. Until then, she had kept them in her bedroom, where she read them at night after going to bed. Now, she left the books and pamphlets on the coffee table and read them in the living room. Her sons seemed tense whenever she would pick up one of these books. Finally, the oldest one broke the ice and asked, "Why are you reading that stuff, Mom? You're not an alcoholic." Margaret had her answer ready. She said,

> Because your father was, and because all three of you boys have drinking problems, too, in my opinion. I want to understand

substance abuse better. I've also been seeing someone to get some help in understanding how I can separate myself from your problems and start taking care of myself a little.

After an awkward moment of silence, her son replied that he felt Margaret had been rejecting him and his brothers lately and questioned whether she was being "brainwashed by a shrink." Margaret said she was making her own decisions. "I'm simply learning to let you boys be responsible for yourselves. Of course, I think *you* boys ought to see someone about your drinking or else go to AA. But that's your decision to make. I'm doing this for me."

As the months rolled by, Margaret's self-esteem grew steadily. She started saving the money her sons gave her, continued going to Al-Anon meetings, and proceeded with her plans for retirement. She made a point of not keeping this secret: She had a realtor come and give her an estimate of how much she could expect to sell the house for and a retirement counselor came and spoke with her about managing her income and expenses after retiring.

It was just over a year after Margaret began therapy and started going to Al-Anon that one son—the middle one—signed himself into an alcohol rehabilitation program. Two months later, her oldest son told her he'd started going to AA meetings with his brother. Soon after that, the youngest son—still drinking—moved out of the house. In assessing the way things had gone, Margaret had this to say: "I would never have imagined that things could change so much in my family just by me changing myself."

Example of Caring Detachment: Ron

Ron's case was somewhat less dramatic than Margaret's, but it is just as illustrative of how detaching works. He had been married to Joan for twenty-five years. He had retired from the military two years earlier, and that was when what had been mere suspicion for several years became obvious: His wife had a drinking problem. He brought up the issue once or twice, but each time, she had reacted with anger. Being a man who disliked intense conflict in his personal relationships, he dropped the subject rather than risking a blowup.

Ron explained that Joan started drinking wine every day at about three or four in the afternoon. By dinnertime, she had pretty much finished off a bottle. Despite this, Ron described their life together as generally good. They were pretty active and healthy and had a lot of friends with whom they socialized. Aside from Joan's tendency to be irritable on occasion, the only major complaint he had was that she would usually fall asleep on the couch by nine at night. Before he retired, Ron thought this was just because she was tired, but now he knew the truth, and he admitted it bothered him. "It gets kind of lonely and boring being up by yourself every night," he said. "And knowing that it's due to her drinking makes it all the more annoying."

Joan tried to rationalize her problem away by saying it was "just wine" she was drinking. "I don't touch hard liquor and you know it!" she shot back once when Ron very tentatively brought up the issue of drinking. He had gone to a few Al-Anon meetings, and he recognized her response as denial at work. He heard stories about how inventive alcoholics could be when it came to finding excuses to drink and also how defensive they could be when it came to minimizing the extent that alcohol was affecting their lives.

Ron's detachment came in a very simple but ultimately very effective form. It seemed that he also enjoyed wine but only with dinner, and he drank moderately—rarely more than two glasses a night and usually only one. He still enjoyed it, but he confessed that ever since he realized that Joan was getting drunk almost every day, his pleasure had diminished considerably. Naturally, Joan encouraged his drinking, because it provided a convenient cover for her own. She would even suggest that they go shopping together to look for good wine values.

Eventually, Ron came to appreciate how his own wine drinking constituted a signal to Joan: "Everything's okay, go ahead and drink." When he realized the role that he was unwittingly playing in his wife's substance abuse problem, he became even more uncomfortable with their nightly dinner rituals. He finally decided he would stop. He told Joan that he was not happy with himself about drinking every day and wanted to change his pattern. He would drink, he said, occasionally over a meal, but he had decided to largely forego it as a daily event. She could drink if she chose to, he said, but most of the time he would not.

Predictably, Joan reacted strongly. She accused Ron of "moralizing" about drinking, and she said he was giving up drinking in an attempt to "control" her. Ron was ready for this. He replied that Joan was an adult, and he reiterated that she was free to make her own decisions about drinking. But he was also an adult and was making his own decision.

For the next several weeks, Ron reported to his counselor that he and Joan fought more than they had in their whole marriage, not necessarily over drinking but over little things. At the same time, he noticed that Joan drank less in the afternoon. Although she continued to drink wine with dinner even when he did not, she drank less then too. This new pattern continued for several months. Ron was resistant about going back to Al-Anon, but he stuck by his decision to change his own behavior; in fact, his own drinking decreased even more over time. Meanwhile, he increased his exercising and, overall, felt much healthier.

The cases described illustrate how detaching affects both the codependent and the substance abuser. Although in both cases the substance abusers changed, learning to detach clearly improved the overall mental health of the significant others. Detaching involves allowing a substance abuser to experience the natural consequences of his or her problem, but clearly, effective detaching also goes well beyond this.

In part 2 of this book, the reader will be given more specific direction in facilitating caring detachment. It is a process that encompasses both behaviors and attitudes, and it can become a powerful force for change in the substance abuser–codependent relationship.

Chapter 5 || Recovery and the Process of Group Bonding

The Importance of Fellowship

Actively facilitating significant others' involvement in Twelve Step fellowships is a powerful way to help those individuals deal with the impact that addiction has had on them and their families. The understanding, encouragement, and support that fellowship provides is a balm for the wounded self-esteem, hopelessness, and chronic anxiety that many significant others suffer. Secondarily, involvement in Al-Anon or Nar-Anon, and specifically learning to develop a relationship with the substance abuser that is based on caring detachment rather than enabling, can be a potent means of motivating a substance abuser to change. Over the long run, the most appropriate and effective agent of change for the loved ones of substance abusers is to be found through bonding to a supportive group of people who find themselves confronting similar issues.

To achieve these goals, the therapist needs to understand the process by which an individual goes from being a nonmember of a mutual-help group to an individual who could be said to be bonded to it and committed to following its program in day-to-day life. That process, of course, begins by attending meetings.

Participation in Al-Anon or Nar-Anon

Bonding begins with being there. For that reason, attending Al-Anon or Nar-Anon meetings is a repeated recommendation, or recovery task, in the FRP. It is helpful for the therapist to be familiar with the format of the group a client is being referred to so the client can be prepared. Knowing in advance what to expect when one first walks into an Al-Anon or Nar-Anon meeting can help put the client at ease and facilitate his or her introduction to a mutual-help fellowship. Clients who are prone to social anxiety, who express exceptional guilt and shame in connection with their loved ones' substance abuse problems, or who worry about potential exposure may hesitate to take even the first step toward using a mutual-help group, which, of course, is getting to a meeting.

Al-Anon, Nar-Anon, and other Twelve Step meetings can vary considerably in format. So-called *open meetings* are open to persons who do not necessarily have a loved one with an alcohol or drug problem, whereas *closed meetings* are to be attended only by men and women who acknowledge being in such relationships. Regardless of the type, meetings last from an hour to an hour and a half. Time is set aside for socializing and networking (e.g., getting phone numbers or e-mail addresses, approaching potential sponsors) either before or after the formal meeting. Each meeting has a chairperson who is elected by the group and, usually, a secretary. These offices and responsibilities typically change hands periodically.

Descriptions of some of the different types of Twelve Step meetings follow:

Speaker Meeting

At these meetings, which are highly recommended for newcomers, members of the group and occasionally "guest speakers" relate the stories of their experiences with addiction and recovery. The format of these stories is as follows: how things were, what happened, how things are now. This is the core story of addiction and recovery, and it is ultimately the basis for bonding. Occasionally, an Al-Anon group will invite a recovering alcoholic or addict to tell his or her story of addiction and recovery. Most often, though, it is group members who share their personal stories of how they learned to move away from enabling toward caring detachment and what that change did for them.

Discussion Meeting

The format here is to select a topic (e.g., gratitude, shame, grief, detachment, enabling, resentments) and to share one's thoughts about it. Typically, either the chairperson selects the topic or the members do so in rotation. Sometimes, the topic is a reading from *Al-Anon Faces Alcoholism, One Day at a Time in Al-Anon,* or another AA, Al-Anon, Nar-Anon, or NA publication.[1] Even simply listening at discussion meetings can help to instill renewed hope in a newcomer, help him or her to see the relationship with the substance abuser from a new perspective, and desensitize the shame and guilt that are often associated with addiction.

Step Meeting

In Step meetings, one of the Twelve Steps is read and then members share their thoughts about how they as individuals are "working" that Step: how they are attempting to implement it in their day-to-day lives and particularly in their relationships with the substance abusers. Newcomers have an opportunity at Step meetings to learn how others have interpreted the Steps and how they relate to the lifestyle and attitude changes that are associated with caring detachment and recovery. Some Step meetings limit themselves to the first three Steps, whereas others include all Twelve Steps as topics for reflection and discussion.

TREATMENT NOTE

Reassuring the Nervous Newcomer

It is said within Twelve Step fellowships that "the most important person in a meeting is the newcomer." Virtually all Twelve Step meetings take pains to greet newcomers and to make them feel welcome. Al-Anon, for example, has this to say:

> The newcomer to Al-Anon usually feels alone in a hostile world, drowning in a sea of troubles. To be sure, some may have been of her own making, but all of us had much to learn about living with an alcoholic before we could begin to create a serene and orderly world within us. Let us not be too eager to swamp this confused person with advice. A warm welcome and words of hope and reassurance will be all the therapy she can use at first. One member, too, should offer a protecting wing and a willing ear to her troubles if she cares to talk about them after the meeting.[2]

The therapist should be aware of this tradition of welcoming (but not pressuring) newcomers. It stems from an even more fundamental Twelve Step Tradition: that it should be *attraction*, as opposed to *promotion*, that draws individuals to the fellowship.[3] The newcomer can therefore be assured that she or he will not be unduly pressured to sign up or commit. Those unfamiliar with Twelve Step fellowships commonly harbor such expectations, and they can be one reason a client may be reluctant to give Al-Anon or Nar-Anon a try. It is often helpful to ask the client to share whatever fears or negative expectations he or she may have and then to share the information just given about what the client can more likely expect when going to a meeting.

Those being referred to meetings for the first time are helped if the therapist can provide them with a current meeting schedule. If the therapist cannot get a schedule, information about meetings is usually available through a public information service line (listed in most local telephone books) or via the Internet (www.al-anon.alateen.org or www.nar-anon.org). Published and posted schedules list the times and places of all meetings and also indicate what type of meetings they are and whether there are any restrictions (e.g., nonsmoking, women only).

In addition to the generic types of meetings are a growing number of specialty meetings: men's meetings, women's meetings, meetings for seniors, meetings for parents, and so forth. The formats of all meetings tend to be informal: Members can elect to speak or simply to listen, and they can leave whenever they choose.

Whatever particular group the therapist is attempting to use as part of FRP treatment, educating the significant other about what to expect can facilitate the person's initial involvement. Also, specific therapeutic interventions, such as simple encouragement, making specific suggestions ("Just go and listen the first few times"), problem-solving (e.g., transportation or child care issues), and even role-playing ("Let's practice how you can introduce yourself") can all be brought to bear toward the end of helping the client get started with a Twelve Step group.

Identification

The process of bonding is facilitated when the newcomer is able to identify with other members of the group. The telling of personal stories is a strong tradition within Twelve Step fellowships and forms the basis for identification. Listening to stories of addiction and recovery—how it was, what happened, how it is now—is a concrete means through which newcomers can feel connected to others. The ability to experience commonality in this way bridges differences in sex, ethnicity, and other factors that might otherwise undermine the bonding process. It helps to define the commonalities that bring people together, despite their many other differences. These commonalities include not only typical relationship issues, such as conflicts with the substance abuser over money or responsibilities, but also personal issues, such as chronic worry over what will happen to the family if the codependent begins to detach or guilt associated with fears that the codependent may have somehow caused the problem.

"Identify, don't compare" is the advice often given to the AA newcomer. The same would be true for the newcomer to Al-Anon or Nar-Anon. The therapist can expect to encounter more or less resistance to this idea of identifying with others, and the more that resistance can be worked through, the more the client can be expected to begin to bond with the group. Most often resistance at this stage takes the form of the client drawing contrasts between himself or herself and others in the group, as opposed to focusing on commonalities. These contrasts may be based on age, sex, education, occupational class, religiosity, income, and even interests. The motivation behind drawing such contrasts quickly becomes apparent: The anxious or uncomfortable client emphasizes differences to resist identifying with the group and as a means to justify rejecting it. She or he is avoiding the bonding process.

For the addict, bonding occurs when the newcomer to AA or NA identifies with the core story of Alcoholics Anonymous, which is a story of a journey from powerlessness and hopelessness to empowerment and renewal through commitment to "a new community of interpretation and action."[4] So it is for the significant other. A comparable theme—of a journey from despair to renewal—applies to the journey that the loved ones of substance abusers face. The resistant alcoholic or addict rejects the notion of powerlessness and clings instead to an illusion that personal willpower alone will succeed in controlling substance use. Similarly, codependents often resist the idea that their love and willpower is not enough to overcome the substance abuse problems. Of course, by clinging to this idea, most codependents unwittingly enable the problem to continue.

Many substance abusers, as well as many significant others, initially balk at the mere mention of the word *powerlessness*. It has been pointed out, however, that there is "a kind of power that issues from acknowledged powerlessness."[5] That power has its roots in collective identification and bonding: in the strength that comes from having the humility to accept personal limitation and the faith that comes from a willingness to trust others and follow the collective wisdom of those who have made the same journey. To the extent that the therapist can help the resistant client identify with key elements of other members' stories, she or he also indirectly helps to empower that client.

Networking

Networking is an integral part of all Twelve Step fellowships. All groups strongly encourage members to build a support network by establishing contact with other members on a regular basis. AA calls this *telephone therapy*.[6] It is equally encouraged in Al-Anon and Nar-Anon. Today, networking is easily extended beyond telephone therapy, including the use of e-mail, texting, and online chat rooms. The therapist should take pains to encourage significant others to network with others in any or all of these ways. The purpose of such networking is to establish a "safety net" in advance of the need for one: to have a network of friends already in place if a crisis occurs or to use them as a sounding board when trying to decide what to do in a given situation.

Building a network can be critical as the client begins to take those first, usually tentative, steps to detach from the addict. Through networking and personal contact before or after meetings, the newcomer begins to make new friends and establish himself or herself in a new peer group—one that is moving away from codependence toward a healthier way of relating to the substance abuser.

Sponsorship

Sponsorship is unique to Twelve Step fellowships. It had its origins in recovering alcoholics who were willing to assume responsibility for taking detoxified alcoholics to meetings when those alcoholics were discharged from hospitals.[7] Those earliest sponsors often had little more sobriety than the men they were sponsoring. From those beginnings, the role of the sponsor evolved into that of guide and mentor. The relationship of the "sponsee" to the sponsor is an important one, especially so for the newcomer. An effective sponsor is an invaluable asset to the newcomer. Without a sponsor as a resource, the client is apt to turn to the therapist for advice and support when that advice and support could be obtained through the Al-Anon or Nar-Anon fellowships. The therapist should, therefore, consistently encourage and, if necessary, coach the client regarding how to find and use an initial (temporary) Al-Anon or Nar-Anon sponsor.

As a rule, the sponsor should either be someone of the same sex as the client or at least someone not likely to develop a romantic interest in the client. A sponsor should also be someone who is active in the fellowship and who has established some clear detachment from the alcoholic or addict in his or her own life. Finally, the sponsor should be someone who possesses what the client perceives to be a good—indeed even admirable—character and who leads a healthy lifestyle that the client would like to emulate in at least some ways.

In monitoring whether the newcomer-sponsor relationship is working well, the therapist should inquire as to how often the newcomer speaks to or otherwise contacts the sponsor (often, one hopes) and whether the sponsor is making specific suggestions about meetings, detaching, and so on. A sponsor is *not* a therapist, however, and a good sponsor will limit the relationship to what he or she knows best, which is how to use the resources of Al-Anon and Nar-Anon and how to work the Twelve Step program one day at a time. Developing a relationship with a sponsor constitutes an important step toward bonding with the fellowship.

Rituals and Traditions

Participation in rituals and traditions have always represented a vehicle whereby the individual bonds to a group. Families stay connected in part through their rituals and traditions. Twelve Step fellowships, including Al-Anon and Nar-Anon, are also rich in rituals and traditions that bond members together. The newcomer who is ambivalent about the group can be expected to be uncomfortable with rituals and, therefore, reluctant to participate in them wholeheartedly at first. Typical rituals include reciting the "Serenity Prayer" as a group, acknowledging and celebrating members' anniversaries of active membership, storytelling, holiday celebrations, and so on.

Other traditions that newcomers can partake of include what is called *service work*: setting up chairs, making coffee, and cleaning up after meetings. These simple contributions to the group can help to bond the newcomer to it over time and should be encouraged. Newcomers who are socially shy and inclined to be quiet listeners at meetings can begin to bond through volunteering for service work.

Because AA and other Twelve Step fellowships are intentionally decentralized, many individual groups develop their own unique rituals and traditions. The therapist is likely to learn of these from the newcomer who reports back on his or her latest experiences with the group. By understanding the important role that these rituals and traditions play in cementing the relationship to the group and encouraging the newcomer to give it a try and keep an open mind, the therapist can play a significant role in transferring the locus of therapeutic change from the client-therapist relationship to the client-group relationship.

The foregoing has been a brief look at the process by which a newcomer to Al-Anon or Nar-Anon can be helped to bond to those fellowships. This is not a passive process, and the more active the therapist can be in promoting it, the more likely it is that his or her client will make the connections necessary to support the process of detachment.

Chapter 6 || Getting What You Wish For

Family Issues in Early Recovery

There is an old saying that goes something like this: "Be careful what you wish for, for you just might get it." Perhaps this is intended as a warning to the chronically malcontent or perhaps it is a message about appreciating what we have. In either case, there is a kernel of wisdom here, in that change—even change we deeply wish for—can sometimes produce results we may not anticipate or necessarily welcome. Certainly, this can be the case when an alcoholic or addict decides abruptly to quit drinking alcohol or using drugs. In this chapter, we will look at some of the issues loved ones might encounter should a substance abuser decide to stop abusing substances.

The Dry Drunk Syndrome

Some substance abusers try to get clean and sober using the "white-knuckle" approach, which means they stop using alcohol or drugs abruptly without any form of outside support from sources such as AA. The effects such a decision has on families and relationships may be much more difficult to endure than the changes that come when a substance abuser decides to commit him or herself to an AA or NA program of recovery as a means to achieve sobriety.

Such a white-knuckle approach can lead to *dry drunk syndrome*,[1] a term coined to refer to a constellation of personality traits associated with someone who decides to give up alcohol or drugs without seeking support and without pursuing or participating in some program of character growth and spiritual renewal, such as a Twelve Step fellowship. These programs were based in part on recognition that the process of addiction has effects on the substance abuser spiritually and psychologically, as well as physically. One clear implication of the Twelve Steps is that involvement in a program such as AA can help to mitigate these effects and spare others the pain of having to live with them. It is a program of character growth and spiritual renewal as much as it is a support system for staying clean and sober.

In *The Dry Drunk Syndrome*, R. J. Solberg discusses dry drunk attitudes:

> Whenever we experience a full-blown dry drunk, we leave the world of sobriety. Our mental and emotional homes become chaotic, our approach to everyday living unrealistic. All this is reflected in our attitudes and actions.[2]

As Jill found, it is not easy for significant others to live with a dry drunk. Jill's husband Kevin had been forced to admit himself to a treatment center after he'd gotten into a car accident—with their two young daughters in the back seat—while driving drunk and stoned on marijuana. Jill had been aware of Kevin's drinking and pot use since they were teenagers. She had taken a tolerant attitude, in part because she felt she had no right to "dictate" to him, and in part because she also had a history of drinking and getting high in her teens and early twenties. But at age thirty-four, Jill had not smoked marijuana in ten years, and her drinking had decreased to the social level, with an occasional glass of red wine over dinner. Kevin, on the other hand, continued to get high every morning before he left for work and drunk every night when he got home. Though his work performance was affected by his substance abuse, he was fortunate in that he worked for a family business where he enjoyed the benefits of a certain degree of toleration born of the family's unwillingness to confront the issue.

All that changed with the accident. With the aid of a counselor, Jill orchestrated a family meeting called an *intervention*. When Kevin entered his parents' family room, he found himself confronted by a united front of family members, along with an addiction counselor and the family's pastor, all of whom insisted they cared about Kevin deeply, and because they cared, they were insisting that he get help for his alcohol and other drug use. They informed him that they made arrangements for him to be admitted to a residential treatment facility for twenty-eight days and they were prepared to drive him there that day. His father told him that if he refused, he'd have to find another job.

Kevin complained bitterly all the way to the treatment center. That night, after being admitted and undergoing a lengthy assessment, he called Jill and described the center as "a Mickey Mouse operation." He complained that he couldn't relate to either the other patients or the counselors. "I need someone who hunts, who runs a business—someone who can relate to my lifestyle," he complained bitterly. He wanted to leave the treatment center after a week, but reluctantly agreed to stay for two.

When Kevin returned home, he told Jill that he realized he did have a drinking problem and that he decided not to drink—"for now." Jill found the "for now" part of this response disconcerting, but she tried to focus on the positive, being grateful at least that Kevin acknowledged he had a problem and wasn't drinking at that point.

Three weeks passed, and Kevin stuck to his word about not drinking. But Jill was finding it hell to live with him. She said:

> He's angry all the time. When he gets home, I just try to keep the kids out of his way. I try to stay out of his way, too. He hardly talks to any of us. He just keeps himself busy all the time. And he hasn't approached me once for sex—not that I'm feeling all that turned on to him. I can't tell you how tense it is with him around. He acts like he's suffering so. He definitely was easier to live with when he was smoking pot and drinking every day. Not that I want to go back to that. I definitely don't. On the other hand, when family asks how things are going, I just tell them he isn't drinking, and they think that's great. They have no idea what our life is like these days!

It would probably be fair to say that Kevin was a dry drunk. Substance abusers who have this syndrome are often

- grandiose, with an exaggerated sense of their own importance
- judgmental, prone to make negative and inappropriate value judgments of others
- intolerant, with little ability to accept differences between themselves and others

- impulsive, heedless of the ultimate consequences of their behavior and unable to delay gratification
- lacking introspection, self-absorbed but unable to view their own behavior objectively or critically[3]

Another way to understand this constellation of personality traits is that, taken together, they reflect a decided immaturity. If one views addiction as a process that is associated psychologically with a slow but steady regression to earlier and less mature levels of development, then one could hypothesize that the adult alcoholic or addict who simply quits is, in psychodynamic terms, like a big child. This is precisely the way Jill perceived Kevin, and she said as much: "I feel like I have *three* kids now, and one of them—Kevin—is just a petulant, self-absorbed, surly adolescent."

Twelve Step fellowships, such as AA and NA, which advocate a program of spiritual renewal and character growth, represent one way that helps substance abusers progress out of the infantile state that addiction has led to. Through involvement in AA or NA, the alcoholic or addict can (and will) be confronted by others who perceive his or her behavior for what it is. For example, Kevin may well have been told to "Get off the pity pot!" in response to his feeling sorry for himself, had he gone to AA. He would also have heard others talk about self-pity, identifying it as a dangerous form of arrogance and one that threatens recovery. But he chose not to go, and so Jill and his two young children were left to deal with him and his ignorance of how much substance abuse had affected him and how much maturing he had to do. They had to live with this man who stalked around the house constantly brimming over with resentment like a charged cloud seeking a target for its lightning.

Fortunately, Jill had started going to Al-Anon when Kevin went into treatment. There, she found people who understood and related to what she was going through and who could share whatever wisdom they had about how they handled similar situations. Beyond that, she discovered a place she could vent the shame she had been experiencing over her secret wish at times that Kevin would go back to drinking, just to reduce the level of tension in the house.

In Al-Anon, Jill found what she called a lifesaving source of sympathy and support. Simply discovering that others had gone through similar experiences and that the dry drunk syndrome was not only real but also common in men like Kevin provided Jill with a deep sense of relief, even as she continued to struggle with the realities of living with Kevin. Regardless of what Kevin decided to do about his drinking and other drug use, she said, she was going to continue going to Al-Anon.

As the case of Jill and Kevin shows, being aware of the dry drunk syndrome can be very useful for the therapist who will have to work with the loved ones of alcoholics or addicts who get sober, especially if they decide to do so without going to AA or NA. There is a good chance that coping with sobriety will be harder for loved ones to deal with if the alcoholic or addict decides to rely on willpower alone instead of using AA or NA as a means of staying clean and sober. In such cases, the prognosis for recovery may be poorer as well. In Kevin's case, for example, he "decided" to have some wine after about a month of sobriety. From his point of view, that month of sobriety had proven that he could control his drinking. He, therefore, saw no further need to abstain. Within another month, however, he was back to drinking not only wine but also bourbon (his drink of choice) before dinner. He pointed out defensively to Jill that he now drank only one bourbon on the rocks, whereas before he would have three or four before dinner. A month after that, Jill, looking for a toy that her oldest daughter had misplaced, happened to open a cabinet in their living room. She reached in and, to her surprise, pulled out a half gallon of bourbon, half empty, which she knew had not been there a week earlier.

As Kevin continued down the slippery slope into relapse, Jill continued going to Al-Anon and staying in touch with several of the women she met there. She got ongoing support for her efforts to resist enabling Kevin while detaching from him. Part of this new behavior involved telling family members to talk to Kevin directly about whether he was or wasn't drinking and telling Kevin that if he ever drove again after drinking with either of their daughters in the car, she would separate from him. She told this to

Kevin when he was sober, and she explained that it had been a difficult decision for her to make. She wanted Kevin to know, however, that she was serious about it. She hoped it would never come to that point, she explained, but she loved both Kevin and her children and would not risk losing all of them in an alcohol-related car accident.

Relational Land Mines: Things to Watch Out For

Attempts by significant others to get a substance abuser sober invariably create emotional ripples within that relationship—indeed, within the family as a whole. Descriptions follow of some of the issues the therapist may encounter.

Monitoring

Monitoring refers to any and all attempts to keep track of how much an alcoholic is drinking or an addict is using. Marking bottles of liquor or wine, and counting or weighing the user's supply of marijuana, are examples of this behavior. Monitoring is a common and natural reaction to a substance abuse problem. It often leads to a good deal of nagging on the part of the client and defensive anger (or unexpressed resentment) on the part of the substance abuser. The goal of monitoring is obvious: It is an attempt to get the drinker to drink less or the drug user to use less by letting him or her know that you know how much he or she is drinking or using.

Spouses and other loved ones who have engaged in monitoring say that it sometimes leads to a temporary reduction in substance abuse, despite the anger it provokes. This may occur because the substance abuser desires to minimize such confrontations by placating the significant other or it may reflect guilt or shame on the part of the substance abuser. The fact that it may initially produce such effects may reinforce monitoring behavior in the loved ones of substance abusers.

Although monitoring may have an effect on drinking or drug use, that effect is typically transient. Sooner or later, as was the case with Kevin, the alcoholic or addict will react to it by hiding the supply of drugs or alcohol, by drinking or using in secret, or both.

Alternatively, the substance abuser may eventually become more or less immune to the loved one's nagging. This, in turn, leads to frustration and eventually to feelings of failure, hopelessness, and depression in the significant other, to shame and resentment in the substance abuser, and to alienation in the relationship.

Behaviorally oriented interventions, as well as the present Twelve Step–oriented program, agree that this form of monitoring should be avoided. The exception might be a case in which a loved one has avoided sharing his or her concern about the substance abuser's drinking or drug use. In that instance, the conspiracy of silence could be construed as enabling on the part of the significant other—in other words, as giving tacit approval to substance abuse. In this instance, the therapist might consider coaching the client on how to break that conspiracy. Even so, ground rules for doing so would include confronting the substance abuser only when he or she is sober, doing so in as calm a manner as possible, and avoiding blowups. The loved one is also admonished to avoid ongoing monitoring and any tendency to nag at the substance abuser, because those actions almost always prove counterproductive.

From the Twelve Step perspective, monitoring the substance abuser when he or she is sober is no more desirable than doing so when he or she is using for several reasons. Here is where behavioral approaches and Twelve Step philosophy diverge, for behaviorists would argue that significant others should continue to monitor and reinforce reduced drinking or using through praise, favors, and other rewards.[4] From the perspective of Al-Anon, however, this would constitute a continuance of the loved one taking responsibility for the substance abuser's behavior. The goal of Al-Anon is to allow each partner—the substance abuser and the codependent—to be responsible for (and therefore to take credit for) his or her own recovery. Al-Anon and Nar-Anon clearly emphasize caring detachment as the healthiest model for a relationship. Consequently, they would no more advocate ongoing monitoring with reinforcement than they would advocate ongoing monitoring with punishment as a desirable dynamic in a relationship with an addict. The therapist using the

FRP model would, therefore, be working most consistently with Al-Anon or Nar-Anon philosophy by being cautious about advocating any form of monitoring at all, be it accompanied by punishment or reward or not.

That is not to say that some recognition of a substance abuser's sobriety is inappropriate. On the other hand, systematic monitoring with an eye toward behavior modification goes well beyond mere recognition. Moreover, the recovering person will most assuredly receive much recognition from his or her fellow substance abusers through involvement in AA or NA. This connection to a fellowship of recovering persons, not the relationship of the substance abuser with the loved one, should be the primary source of reinforcement for the recovering substance abuser.

Resentments

Addiction leads to alienation in relationships. Men and women who progressively lose a loved one to alcoholism or drug addiction typically go through a process that begins with anxiety and concern, proceeds through frustration and anger, and ends in despair and alienation. Along the way, the loved ones of substance abusers are likely to experience deep senses of failure (in arresting the addiction), along with deep resentments of the alcohol or drugs (or both) that have destroyed the relationships. It is no surprise, then, that clients may find themselves experiencing not only joy but anger and resentment when their loved ones do get clean and sober. The therapist should be prepared to hear and deal with such feelings. The goal is to help to desensitize the shame or guilt that is associated with such feelings.

The most helpful initial response to anger in a loved one of a substance abuser who is new to recovery is for the therapist to react with understanding (i.e., to normalize it). This can provide a great deal of relief to the clients who may feel shame that they are angry instead of happy that their loved ones are finally making an effort to stay clean or sober. Because many clients may have such feelings (and be ashamed of them), the therapist would do well to bring up the subject. When doing so, the best approach is to indicate that such feelings are common enough as to be the rule rather than the exception. Open-ended questions preceded by a brief introduction, such as the following, can be useful in testing for resentment and shame:

- Addiction stirs up many reactions in people, such as yourself, who are close to a substance abuser. We can feel worried and anxious when we first realize that our loved one has a problem. Usually, we try our best to get them to stop. This leads to frustration and anger and, sometimes, to a sense of failure. Eventually, we can feel very alienated and hopeless. Have you ever experienced any of these feelings in your relationship?
- When an alcoholic or addict first gets into recovery, we want to be happy for him or her, and of course, part of us is. But then, there are still all those leftover feelings—hopelessness, anger, resentment—that we've had to more or less stuff so long as he or she was drinking or using. Often these feelings never see the light of day while the substance abuser is actively drinking or using; then we may experience them when he or she gets sober. This can be very upsetting, but it's a common reaction and really very understandable. Have you found yourself having any feelings of anger or resentment now that your loved one has stopped drinking or using?
- What have you tried to do to deal with any resentment, frustration, or anger you have that's left over from when ______________ was actively drinking or using? Have you felt uncomfortable or ashamed at any time over any of these feelings?

Once feelings of resentment are acknowledged, the issue then becomes how to deal with them and how to communicate them to the substance abuser. This issue is best approached as a collaborative effort between the client and the therapist. It is not necessarily easy for an alcoholic or addict to hear these feelings from his or her loved ones, but sooner or later he or she needs to hear them, lest they fester and undermine the relationship. The Twelve Step program of recovery includes explicit provisions for acknowledging harm done to others as a result of addiction and the need to make appropriate amends for such acts. Reassuring significant others that their feelings are understandable and normal—and that they can also reasonably expect that the substance abuser will at some point hear them out and make amends—can help turn destructive resentment into a productive exchange between the substance abuser and the significant other. However, it is also important to keep in mind that the substance abuser may not be best able to accept or deal with a loved one's anger very early in his or her recovery. It may have to be sufficient for a time for significant others to share these feelings with the therapist and with others at Al-Anon or Nar-Anon meetings.

The following are offered as guidelines for discussing the issue of resentment and how to resolve it:

- Do you think it would it help if you could express any feelings of anger or resentment you have about having lost ______________ to addiction directly to him (her)?
- How would you express your resentment? What exactly would you like to say to ______________?
- When do you think would be the best time for you to sit down with ______________ and express some of these feelings you have about his (her) addiction and the effect it has had on you and on your relationship? Do you think you should do this soon? If not, at what point in ____________'s recovery would you do it?

Properly done, helping a significant other to unburden himself or herself of long-standing resentments can open the door to true reconciliation in the substance abuser–codependent relationship. Ironically, many relationships seem to fail not while a substance abuser is actively using but after she or he gets sober. One reason for this may have to do with this issue of unresolved resentments.

Jealousy

"Before he got sober, he spent all his time drinking. Now that he's sober, he spends all his time at AA meetings!" Such sentiments have been expressed by more than one spouse or child of a recovering alcoholic or addict, and they are understandable. Consider, for example, the implications for a newly recovering substance abuser's relationships with family members of the common AA prescription to newcomers to attend ninety meetings in ninety days. An old saw within AA and NA, this "90 in 90" advice turns out to have a sound empirical basis because most relapses have been found to occur within the first ninety days after a substance abuser stops drinking or using other drugs.[5] At the same time that it makes sense in terms of recovery, though, this "90 in 90" rule can effectively mean that the recovering person may spend more time at meetings during this period than she or he does at home.

In addition to being asked to attend as many as ninety meetings in ninety days, the newcomer to AA or NA will be encouraged to stay after meetings to talk, to go out for coffee with others after meetings, to spend time talking to other AA members on the phone or via e-mail, to get a sponsor and maintain frequent contact with him or her, to read the Big Book and other literature, and so on. Although all these activities make sense in terms of getting a good start on recovery, taken together, they also mean that the newly recovering person may seem, from the point of view of family members, to have "traded one addiction (alcohol or drugs) for another (AA or NA)," as one spouse put it.

The therapist should be prepared to empathize with the significant other who expresses the sentiment that he or she has in essence "lost" the substance abuser again—this time to a Twelve Step fellowship. Often these loved ones have longed for years to have better relationships with the substance abusers. They may be reluctant to admit that they are in fact jealous of the recovering person's newfound relationships within AA or of the fact that these other anonymous people seem able to do what they were not (i.e., get their loved ones sober).

It would not be abnormal if spouses and other family members were inwardly conflicted about their own emotional reactions to the substance abusers' involvements in Twelve Step fellowships. Almost all concerned significant others truly want to support recovery and may, therefore, be ashamed of any jealousy they experience. As one husband said, "What Joan is doing [staying sober] is what I've wanted, prayed, and hoped for, for years. It bothers me that I feel annoyed when she has to leave every night, and most weekend mornings, to go to meetings. She seems genuinely happy—happier than I've ever seen her—and I want to be happy for her. But sometimes, I know that I'm forcing my smile just a bit, and that I sometimes want to protest about her being gone all the time."

This husband's statement captures the internal conflict experienced by many family members when they first get what they've wished for: their loved one in recovery. Their inner turmoil can easily be misinterpreted as ambivalence about the substance abusers' sobriety itself. Therapists may be tempted to conclude that the significant other would actually prefer the addict or alcoholic to continue drinking or using other drugs. This misperception has led therapists at times to theorize about some secondary gain that significant others derive from addiction and even to suggest that significant others encourage addictive behavior because of this secondary gain. But this is almost always a mistake. More often ambivalence reflects a normal human response—jealousy—to having a relationship diluted by a loved one's intense involvement in some other activity. This can be especially true when a significant other has already lost a loved one to addiction for a prolonged period of time.

When working with family members of substance abusers, it can be helpful to raise and discuss this issue of jealousy, even while the substance abuser is still actively using, in anticipation of what the significant other might experience if the substance abuser became clean and sober. For many significant others, having therapists predict such reactions helps to normalize them and minimize subsequent feelings of guilt.

Certainly, it is appropriate to bring up this issue early in recovery if it hasn't been brought up before. If possible, this should be done with both the recovering substance abuser and the significant other(s) in a family session. Again, frank acknowledgement can help to normalize such feelings and reduce shame and guilt in those significant others who are experiencing them. It can also open a constructive dialogue about the importance of becoming active in a Twelve Step fellowship while not forgetting about the importance of family relationships.

If for some reason the substance abuser is not available for a discussion of this issue with the significant other in a conjoint session, the therapist may want to use a cognitive role-playing technique with the significant other alone. Present the following scenario, and then discuss how the significant other might feel and how she or he might respond if this situation were to arise.

Once your loved one makes a decision to get sober through AA, you might discover that she or he is suddenly going to meetings five to seven times a week, talking to other AA members every night on the phone, spending time having coffee with a sponsor, and talking a lot about AA. Although we both know very well that you want your loved one to get sober, it wouldn't be unusual for you to have a reaction to him or her getting so absorbed in AA:

- How do you think you might feel in this situation?
- If you have children, how do you think they might respond?
- How would you talk to your recovering loved one about your feelings?
- What would you expect from him (her) in terms of attention to your own relationship and family?

Coping with Getting What You Wish For

The alcoholic or addict who decides to get sober and commit to a Twelve Step fellowship will often experience an initial wave of relief. Early recovery, with its promise of renewed hope, along with the sense of physical well-being that comes with sobriety, can create what has been called a "pink cloud of optimism." It is like viewing the world through rose-colored glasses. Soon enough, however, the reality sinks in: Recovery means hard work. As one counselor, in recovery herself, explained it to her client, "Recovery means more than just putting the plug in the jug. It means learning to live life and to live it on life's terms."

The point of this discussion has been that recovery, along with its blessing of sobriety, often brings with it changes that the loved ones of substance abusers may not have anticipated. Recovery can stir up long-suppressed feelings of anger and resentment or it can create jealousy in significant others. A loved one's initial response to early recovery may be something akin to the pink cloud that the substance abuser experiences. Soon enough, however, this will wear off. The therapist is wise to expect this and to prepare the client for it in advance, whenever possible.

Substance abusers in early recovery can be exuberant; sometimes, they can also turn into proselytizers for Twelve Step fellowships. Persons who discover hope for themselves through AA or NA, and who see in the Twelve Steps a true pathway to spiritual renewal, may want to "share" their new discovery with family members, some of whom may be a good deal less enthusiastic about the idea than the substance abuser is. The best advice to give to both the substance abuser and his or her loved ones in early recovery is to encourage acceptance and tolerance: Let the substance abuser pursue his or her program, while the rest of the family members pursue whatever routes feel best for them. For many, Al-Anon will help a great deal, if they are willing to give it a try.

Advocating that family members take a "live and let live" approach to early recovery can help to minimize resentments that could eventually sabotage recovery for all. The FRP is, of course, designed to help the professional counselor facilitate recovery for the whole family using the Twelve Step approach. But it is important that the counselor also takes an attitude of tolerance and understands the kinds of reactions that codependents may have when loved ones first get sober. The therapist should proselytize no more than should the recovering addict. Maintaining this attitude is vital if one hopes to persuade one or more family members to try out the attitudes and behaviors—in particular, caring detachment—that are advocated here.

Part 2 || Facilitating Twelve Step Family Recovery

Program Overview

Part 2 of this book presents, in an extended manual form, a program for therapists working with concerned significant others of substance abusers. It is presented in this way intentionally so it may be used as a guide in planning and conducting treatment. It is supplemented by reproducible session guidelines that are contained on a separate CD-ROM that accompanies this book. It is recommended that therapists print out and use those guidelines when conducting actual individual or group treatment sessions. The guidelines provide the therapist with a handy and accessible step-by-step summary of the sessions, more thoroughly discussed here and in the following chapters.

In addition to the guidelines, the CD-ROM also includes handouts that link to the eight core topics covered in the Family Recovery Program (FRP). These handouts highlight the reading assignments for each session and include "homework" exercises for the client that serve as a review of the material covered for a specific topic and as an opportunity to explore this material on a deeper level.

Early FRP prototypes presented here have been used in randomized clinical trials with spouses, parents, grandparents, adult children, and cohabiting significant others of substance abusers. The program has not been used with minor children of substance abusers. This program is designed to initiate a process of positive change in the family system through a brief, focused intervention with one or more family members. To be effective, the intervention should, therefore, be used only with concerned significant others who have frequent contact with the substance abuser. Because the FRP seeks to accomplish its goals in a relatively brief time, it is also important that the therapist adhere to the treatment protocol as much as possible and avoid drifting into collateral issues. In clinical trials, the FRP has been implemented in twelve sessions spaced over a period as long as six months.

The FRP begins with an assessment session. For some clients, a single hour may be sufficient to complete the assessment process;

on the other hand, it is not unusual for the assessment process to extend over two sessions.

As outlined in the introduction to this book, the FRP program is presented as a series of topics. Like the assessment, many of these topics could be subjects of more than one treatment session. The issue of detaching versus enabling, for example, is apt to be a topic for discussion, coaching, and therapeutic work in virtually every session.

Substance abusers who seek treatment as a result of this intervention with their significant others may be referred to professionals who are prepared to facilitate their involvement in AA or NA (or both). *The Twelve Step Facilitation Outpatient Program* and *Twelve Step Facilitation for the Dually Diagnosed Client* are two such treatment programs.[1] Twelve Step Facilitation has undergone peer review and has been selected for inclusion in the National Registry of Evidence-based Programs and Practices (NREPP) as a treatment that has been evaluated via comparative effectiveness research (CER).

Chapter 7 || Getting Started

Topic 1: Introduction and Assessment

This initial session of the Family Recovery Program (FRP) has an exceptionally large agenda and may take more than the usual hour-long therapy session to complete. Its objectives are as follows:

- to establish rapport between the client and the therapist
- to identify any significant barriers to treatment (transportation, child care, etc.)
- to provide an overview of the program
- to obtain an impression, based on information provided by the client, of the extent of his or her loved one's alcohol or drug problem
- to help the client understand what stage his or her loved one's drinking or drug problem has reached
- to briefly assess the client's own use of alcohol or drugs
- to introduce the first recovery tasks to the client

Introductions

The therapist should be prepared to spend the opening minutes of the initial session just getting acquainted with the significant other. The issue of how the client and therapist will address one another (title and last name versus first name) should be discussed. A point should be made to check whether the meeting time is mutually convenient and whether the client anticipates any transportation problems or other issues (e.g., child care) that might interfere with attendance and that could be worked through at the outset. Such a discussion is helpful in establishing a practical, problem-solving, and collaborative relationship between the client and the therapist.

Presenting a Program Overview

When presenting an overview of the program, it is important that the therapist cover the following points:

Focused Treatment

The therapist should explain that the purpose of the FRP is to assist the significant other in coping more effectively in a relationship with an active substance abuser: to begin the process of healing the negative impact on the significant other that is the result of being in a close relationship with a substance abuser and to alter the relationship with the substance abuser in ways that may eventually motivate the substance abuser to change. Although other issues may arise during this program, some of the therapist's main responsibilities are to follow the prescribed session format and to keep treatment focused on these goals. This focus is not intended to imply that collateral issues are trivial; rather, it is intended to help the client achieve certain specific and limited goals in a brief period of time. Additional therapy may be recommended either following completion of the FRP or collaterally with it. Alternatively, the client may discover ways of dealing with these other issues through the course of the FRP.

Time-Limited Treatment

The FRP was designed to be delivered in approximately twelve individual sessions spaced over a period of up to six months. Though not originally designed as a group intervention, its structure is actually quite amenable to that kind of adaptation. In fact, implementing the FRP in a group format mirrors in many ways the experience clients will have at Al-Anon and Nar-Anon meetings. Group treatment can form a template for group support, which is the main curative factor operating in Twelve Step fellowships.

If further treatment is desired after completion of the FRP, the client is probably best referred to another professional resource for that purpose, so as to preserve the boundaries of this program. Also, it is hoped that as a result of the therapist's efforts, significant others will have developed networks of community-based supportive relationships through Al-Anon or Nar-Anon by the time the program is completed, which can be used as additional sources of nonprofessional help.

It is not recommended that the FRP be extended over a period of time longer than six months or that more than two additional "emergency" sessions be offered. In the event that limited progress has been made and a client wishes to continue, it is suggested that instead of simply continuing, a break of at least three months be taken before resuming treatment. During that time, the client should be encouraged to pursue the same goals on his or her own that are the subject of the FRP: attending Al-Anon or Nar-Anon meetings, establishing a network of contacts via the telephone and e-mail, and establishing a relationship with a sponsor. Progress in these areas should be assessed prior to setting a new therapeutic contract. The therapist needs to be cautious that a client does not merely wish to substitute a professional relationship for active involvement in a Twelve Step fellowship, because this is not likely to prove useful in the long run. Resistance to such involvement is an appropriate subject for any extended sessions.

Role of the Therapist

The significant other needs to know that in the context of the FRP, the therapist is a professional whose expertise is directed at helping that significant other understand addiction and concepts such as codependence, enabling, and detaching, and at facilitating the client's involvement in a Twelve Step fellowship. The therapist is an expert, but the primary means of achieving the program's goals over the long run is ideally to be found through active involvement in Al-Anon or Nar-Anon rather than through the therapeutic relationship alone. This is not to say that the client-therapist relationship is unimportant. On the contrary, clinical experience with this program suggests that without the active support and guidance of the therapist, many clients would either not have tried a Twelve Step fellowship such as Al-Anon or Nar-Anon to begin with or would not have followed through after their initial exposures to one of these fellowships. Rather than minimizing his or her importance as a professional, the therapist using this program believes that bonding to Al-Anon or Nar-Anon represents a long-term solution for the client, whereas the client-therapist relationship is an important but temporary one.

Stages of Substance Use: A Relational Model

The therapist should now present the following *relational model of addiction*. This model describes substance use in terms of a "relationship" between the user and alcohol or drugs and correlates the several stages of addiction with their effects on the substance abuser–codependent relationship.[1] In clinical practice, it has been found that almost all significant others can relate to this idea of addiction as a relationship that proceeds through four stages:

Stage One: Social or Experimental Substance Use

In this stage, the substance user primarily drinks or uses drugs with others. Alcohol and other drugs are used mainly as a social means (to "loosen up" or to "relax") or for their pleasurable effects ("getting high") or both. Although alcohol and other drugs affect the user's emotional state, at this stage these effects tend to disappear as the alcohol or drugs are metabolized. In other words, the user subjectively returns to normal after using. Negative consequences can occur but are relatively rare and may include occasional hangovers or a random DWI arrest. Viewed from a relational perspective, at the social stage of use, alcohol and other drugs can be thought of as *casual friends* of the user.

Substance use at this stage is not generally perceived by loved ones (e.g., spouses or children of the user) or other concerned significant others as threats to their relationships with the substance user. Consequently, substance use at the social or experimental stage is most often met with tolerance or acceptance. The exception might come from a partner who grew up in a nondrinking family, in which case, even social use—if it has any regularity—might be noticed and remarked upon.

Stage Two: Instrumental Substance Use

In this stage, the individual has learned to use alcohol or other drugs *consistently*, either to create certain positive feelings (e.g., relaxation, euphoria) or to avoid certain negative feelings (e.g., anxiety, loneliness). The former pattern is called *hedonistic* use, whereas the latter use is *compensatory* in nature.[2]

Instrumental substance use is the gray area that separates social drinking and other drug use from problem drinking and drug use. Men and women at this stage often begin to drink alcohol or use other drugs alone as well as socially. Relationally speaking, they could be said to have developed a *relationship* with alcohol or other drugs in the sense that their connection to alcohol or other drugs goes beyond a casual level and is not limited to social situations. Use at this stage represents an intentional and consistent effort either to pursue desirable emotional effects (e.g., euphoria, relaxation), to disinhibit certain behaviors (e.g., sex), or to overcome negative emotions (e.g., social anxiety or undesirable behaviors such as shyness or self-consciousness).

Instrumental drinkers or drug users can begin to experience severe negative consequences as a result of their regular use (e.g., cravings or edginess when their substance of choice is not readily available). Despite this, it is unusual for instrumental drug users or drinkers to consider themselves as having a substance use "problem." However, significant others may begin to notice how often the substance users drink or get high and how much they seem to look forward to it. They may also notice the negative behaviors associated with substance users not being able to drink or use other drugs. At this stage, significant others will usually begin to feel uncomfortable about the substance user's drinking or other drug use. Many identify with feeling *jealous* of the deepening "relationship" between the user and his or her substance of choice.

Ironically, significant others who themselves were raised in alcoholic families may fail to react to substance abuse at the instrumental stage. Although one might expect them to have been sensitized by their early experiences, in fact they often have become desensitized by it and are apt to react only when substance abuse has progressed to the next stage: habitual use. In contrast, significant others who were raised in nonaddictive families commonly perceive instrumental use as problematic and react to it as such at this instrumental stage.

This difference in the ways instrumental substance use is perceived by significant others is important clinically, because it may be tempting to pathologize a codependent who appears to take a tolerant attitude toward instrumental substance use. One might hypothesize that he or she unconsciously wants the substance abuser to drink or use, or one might suppose that he or she is unconsciously re-creating his or her family of origin. Before jumping to such conclusions, however, the therapist should consider that what seems like "normal" behavior to an individual depends in large part on the context of that behavior. Social perception, in other words, is contextual. Growing up as a child in a family where shouting and arguing is common, for example, tends to predispose the individual as an adult to perceive verbal fights as essentially nonviolent and no cause for alarm. In contrast, the same individual, after growing up in a conflict-avoidant family, might well perceive a verbal fight as quite violent and disturbing.

Similar contextual factors appear to play a role in determining at what point a significant other will begin to perceive drinking or other drug use as problematic. Contrary to what many may expect, growing up in a family where drinking is commonplace predisposes the individual to not perceive a drinking problem in its early stages. Professionals may be able to promote earlier detection and prevention of addiction by educating significant others in the addiction process and by sensitizing them to cues that are symptomatic of a developing problem, such as instrumental use. To some extent, this is happening now in schools that expose children to drug education programs.

Stage Three: Habitual Substance Use

At this stage, alcohol or drug use has progressed from being a relationship to the level of what could be called a *commitment* that the user has to his or her substance of choice. Loved ones often relate well to this analogy of problem drinking or other drug use as being a "commitment" between the psychoactive substance and the user—a commitment that is not only intimate but one that begins to seriously compete with the user's other relationships and other commitments and responsibilities, such as work.

Children and spouses often experience *resentment* of the habitual user's committed relationship with alcohol or other drugs.

The user now rarely strays far from alcohol or other drugs, and she or he intentionally structures social engagements, vacations, and so on in ways that ensure ready access. As one wife put it, "My husband won't go anywhere without his cooler." And a husband said of his wife, "She refuses to go on a vacation to any place that doesn't have a bar close at hand. I hate cruises; she loves them."

At the habitual stage, negative consequences of use become increasingly apparent, which almost invariably include strained relationships. However, decreased effectiveness at work, financial problems, and declining health may also begin to become evident as habitual use progresses. In addition, definite substance-use-related personality changes begin to appear. In the emotional sphere, these changes most often include a growing emotional instability, increased aggressiveness and irritability, and depression. Psychologically, the habitual user becomes progressively more self-absorbed, unreliable, and demanding—in a word, more regressed.

At the habitual stage of use, significant others experience anger, anxiety, and frustration in attempts to get the user to stop or reliably limit substance use. The user's efforts to control drinking or using amount to little more than a series of false starts ending in failure, the long-term consequence of which is lower self-esteem and increased denial. A parallel process occurs in significant others, who similarly experience failure in their efforts to arrest the problem. Not a few drift into a state of denial as well, essentially looking the other way as the substance abuser slips down the slope into addiction.

Stage Four: Compulsive Substance Use

This is the stage of classic addiction in which substance use has progressed from a commitment to a total preoccupation. At this stage, the relationship between the user and alcohol or other drugs is one of *slave and master*. Psychological and physical dependence now drives the substance user. Staying intoxicated becomes the primary focus of daily living. The compulsive substance user no longer feels normal in the absence of intoxication. Sobriety is associated with acute discomfort and irritability; therefore, intoxication is maintained continuously whenever possible. Negative consequences in terms of health, work, and relationships continue to accrue. The substance abuser is now an extremely regressed, indeed infantile, individual who behaves in a childish manner (e.g., inability to delay gratification, low frustration tolerance, infantile egocentrism, etc.).

By the time substance use has progressed to the compulsive stage, significant others are apt to suffer from deep feelings of *alienation*. Loneliness, depression, hopelessness, and extremely low self-esteem are the most common feelings expressed by significant others of compulsive users when they seek help or first go to an Al-Anon or Nar-Anon meeting.

The therapist will find that the relational model of addiction just described will have particular relevance for many significant others. It should be presented with the aim of helping clients identify where the user is with respect to his or her relationship with alcohol or other drugs and also how the clients have reacted to it. Understanding the course of the significant other's relationship with the substance abuser will provide a useful context for the work on caring detachment that is to follow in later sessions.

Table 7.1 can be a useful visual aid when presenting the relational model of addiction.

Table 7.1
Relational Model of Addiction

Stage of Use	Motivation	"Relationship" to Substance
Social/Experimental	Curiosity Social acceptance	"Casual friend"
Instrumental	Hedonistic: Feel good Compensatory: Avoid feeling bad	"Relationship"
Habitual	Psychological dependency	"Commitment"
Compulsive	Physical dependency	"Slave"

When using the relational model shown in Table 7.1, the therapist should begin by helping the client identify what stage of use the drinker or user is at. Provide Topic 1: Handout 1, Relational Model of Addiction, to your client to facilitate discussion. Talking about the psychological and emotional effects associated with the progression of addiction can help in pinpointing the substance abuser's stage of use.

Next, the therapist should help the client identify how the addiction process has affected his or her relationship with the substance user. Ask the client whether she or he can identify with any of the feelings associated with each stage of use along the progression to addiction (acceptance of early use, jealousy at the instrumental stage, resentment at the habitual stage, alienation at the compulsive stage).

Therapists using this treatment guide are encouraged to frequently use case examples to illuminate the addictive process and its effects on relationships. Here is one such example:

Scott, age sixty-five, had been a self-described "heavy drinker" since late adolescence. He drank heavily and continuously through twenty-odd years of marriage and recalled how his wife once told him that if he agreed to stop drinking and to give her the money, she would buy him a Cadillac at the end of a year. After his wife died, Scott used her death as an excuse to continue drinking, but in truth, he said, he drank no more or no less than ever. Using the relational model as a guide, Scott's therapist established that he had a commitment to alcohol—one that had led in the end to a good deal of resentment on the part of his wife.

A couple of years before seeking help, Scott started dating Rachel, a woman he had met at the local senior center. They were good companions, he said, but he said he had no intention of marrying again: "One time around on the merry-go-round is enough for me." The therapist questioned whether this was the only reason Scott was keeping a distance in this relationship. She established, for example, that Scott had definitely kept the extent of his drinking secret from Rachel. He would drink before they went out, for instance, to get "a head start." He would take her to restaurants that had bars, and usually at least once while they were eating, he excused himself ostensibly to go to the bathroom only to stop for a quick one at the bar before returning to the table. "So it sounds to me like you still have two women in your life, Scott," his therapist said. "You have your girlfriend, Rachel, and you have your 'other girlfriend,' liquor. You take one out for dinner but then you cheat on her even when you're with her." Scott laughed uncomfortably, but he had to admit to the truth of what the therapist was saying: "It's like sneaking off from one lady to kiss another, isn't it?"

After using the relational model to help significant others identify what stage of relationship with alcohol or drugs their substance abusers are at and how it has affected their relationships, ask them to identify at what stage they themselves are with respect to alcohol and drug use and why they believe this to be the case. Be sure to ask the following questions:

- How often do you drink or use drugs? What do you drink or use?
- What is the status of your relationship with alcohol or drugs: casual friend, relationship, commitment, or slave? Has it ever been a stronger relationship than it is today?
- Can you identify any personal negative consequences associated with your use of alcohol or drugs at any time in the past?

Taking a Substance Use History

The next phase of the assessment session consists of gathering a brief history of the substance abuser's use from the point of view of the client, who is the significant other. This is important because the focus of the FRP is on the significant other, not on the substance abuser, so what matters most in the FRP is the client's perspective. Specific areas of inquiry include the *progression* of use, attempts to *stop or control use*, and *negative consequences* associated with use (in both the substance abuser and the client).

Note: Some clinics have reported that devising a questionnaire (see Topic 1: Handout 2, Progression of Substance Use) based on the following questions and asking the client to fill it out in advance of the assessment session, can make the use of this time more efficient as the therapist scans the client's answers and addresses those that stand out.

Progression

The therapist should ask a series of questions aimed at determining how substance use has changed over the course of the relationship. Questions such as the following can be useful in creating a portrait of how far the addiction process has progressed over time. If the therapist has not provided the client with Topic 1: Handout 2, Progression of Substance Use, in advance, he or she can do this now to facilitate the discussion:

- How much did ___(insert person's name)___ drink or use drugs when you first met him or her?
- How frequently did he or she drink or use drugs?
- How often, and how much, does she or he drink or use drugs now?
- When did you first notice that ________ was drinking or using drugs significantly more or more often than he or she did when you first noticed it?
- Can you recall the first time you felt concerned about ________'s substance use? What prompted that concern?
- When was the first time you and ________ had a conflict over his or her substance use? What did you say? How did she or he respond?
- What, if any, significant events were associated with increases in ________'s substance use? For example, were any of the following events associated with increases in substance use?

- ▷ job changes
- ▷ marital conflict
- ▷ losses (deaths, moves, etc.)
- ▷ illnesses
- ▷ traumas (accidents, etc.)
- ▷ financial problems

Attempts to Stop or Control Substance Use

The therapist should now inquire about the significant other's awareness of any efforts that the user has made to stop or control substance use:

- Has (insert person's name) ever tried to stop (or limit) substance use?
- What did she or he do to try to stop (or limit) use?
- How long was she or he successful at not using at all or controlling (limiting) use?
- Has ________ ever gone to AA or NA? How many times?
- What did she or he seem to think of AA or NA?
- Was she or he able to stop or cut down on substance use at that time?
- Have you been aware of any efforts on ________'s part to control substance use?
- Has ________ tried to drink or use drugs only at certain times, such as evenings or weekends, without success?
- Has she or he sworn off certain kinds of alcohol or drugs, again, without success?
- Has ________ ever gone for treatment (either inpatient or outpatient) for his or her substance use problem? If so, when and where? What was the outcome of that treatment?

Inventory of Negative Consequences in the Substance Abuser and the Significant Other

To conclude this succinct alcohol or drug history, the therapist should take some time to construct an inventory of negative consequences that the substance abuser and the significant other have experienced as a result of substance use. To gather this information, the therapist and the client should go through the following list together and discuss to what extent either the substance abuser or the client has experienced any of the following consequences of substance abuse. Give Topic 1: Handout 3, Inventory of Negative Consequences, to your client and ask your client the questions on the following pages to facilitate discussion.

Physical Consequences

Make an effort to identify all medical problems, including accidents or injuries, that have affected the substance abuser, as well as stress-related illnesses that the significant other may have experienced. Discuss which of these problems, in either the substance abuser or the client, could be related in whole or in part to the substance use problem. A partial list of problems to consider includes the following:

	Substance Abuser	**Client**
hypertension or diabetes	_____	_____
gastrointestinal (digestive) problems	_____	_____
sleep disorders (insomnia, restless sleep)	_____	_____
weight loss or gain	_____	_____
auto, home, or job accidents or injuries	_____	_____
injuries suffered as a result of domestic violence	_____	_____
emergency room visits		_____
heart problems	_____	_____

Legal Consequences

Compile a list of all legal consequences correlated with substance use, including but not limited to the following:

	Substance Abuser
DWI arrests	_____
arrests for disorderly conduct (including domestic violence)	_____
arrests for possession of drugs or drug paraphernalia	_____
other ______________________________	_____
other ______________________________	_____

Social Consequences

The therapist should carefully inventory all social consequences of substance use, both to the substance abuser and the client, including these:

	Substance Abuser	Client
loss of friends	_____	_____
alienation from or conflict with family members	_____	_____
marital conflict	_____	_____
child neglect or abuse	_____	_____

Sexual Consequences

Though seldom discussed, substance abuse is commonly associated with sexual dysfunction and other sexual consequences. Ask about sexual dysfunction and other sexual consequences related to substance abuse that have affected the codependent or the substance abuser. These may include the following:

	Substance Abuser	Client
problems of arousal (impotence in men, dyspareunia in women)	_____	_____
orgasmic dysfunction (anorgasmia in women, delayed ejaculation in men)	_____	_____
loss of sexual desire	_____	_____
sexual victimization or exploitation (e.g., rape)	_____	_____

Psychological Consequences for the Significant Other

Ask the significant other about any symptoms of psychological disorder or stress that he or she may be experiencing. Though more inclined by habit to focus on their substance abusers, significant others also commonly experience emotional and psychological problems, such as the following:

	Client
Depression, as reflected in these symptoms:	
irritability or moodiness	_____
hopelessness	_____
loss of motivation	_____
insomnia or disturbed sleep	_____
anxiety attacks	_____
excessive weight gain or loss	_____

Psychological Consequences for Both People

Take an inventory of psychological and emotional problems that the substance abuser and/or the client may be experiencing as a result of substance abuse, including the following:

	Substance Abuser	Client
memory problems (especially forgetfulness)	_____	_____
impulsivity (impulse buying, etc.)	_____	_____
aggressiveness or chronic irritability	_____	_____
impatience and low tolerance for frustration	_____	_____
confused thinking	_____	_____
moodiness and periods of depression	_____	_____

Financial Consequences

Ask the codependent specifically about the impact that substance abuse has had on the substance abuser's and his or her own financial status, including the following:

	Substance Abuser	Client
job problems (losing raises, being fired or placed on probation, being passed over for a promotion)	_____	_____
excessive money spent on alcohol or drugs	_____	_____
out-of-pocket costs for alcohol or drug treatment	_____	_____
credit problems (overextended credit, revoked credit cards, and so forth)	_____	_____
fines and legal fees associated with alcohol- or drug-related arrests	_____	_____

Summing Up

The therapist should use the information gathered through this part of the interview to summarize the impact that substance abuse has had on *both* the user and the significant other. In particular, the therapist should take pains to avoid minimizing in any way the negative impact that substance abuse has had on *the significant other's* physical health, emotional health, sexuality, finances, and so on. This will help to reinforce the need for the significant other to take care of himself or herself.

As a consequence of the insidious, steady *progression* of addiction in the alcohol or drug user—instead of the respective needs of each person in the relationship—becoming the primary focus in the substance abuser–codependent relationship, many codependents develop a long-standing habit of neglecting themselves and their own needs. Many suffer from significant psychological, physical, emotional, and spiritual problems. Failure to clearly point out to the significant other these effects of addiction on him or her may undermine the person's motivation to change his or her ways of relating to the substance abuser, which is central to the FRP. It is often only when (with the help of a therapist) significant others are able to take stock of how substance abuse has affected not only the alcoholic or addict in their lives, but them as well, that many significant others become open to doing something for themselves.

For many clients, being asked to go to meetings, as they are asked to do in the FRP, may be perceived initially as yet another responsibility in what may well be an already overburdened life. Some may regard Al-Anon or Nar-Anon as something else they have to do "for the addict," and therefore, resent it. Again, a primary goal of this program is to shift the focus away from the substance abuser to the significant other, specifically, to his or her physical and mental health, including his or her unmet social needs, in the belief that as a codependent's priorities and behaviors change, so will the substance abuser–codependent relationship.

The summary is a good time to state (or restate) the following points:

- It is important that the significant other focus more on his or her own needs and less on those of the substance abuser. This session should have helped the significant other see how addiction has affected her or him and how she or he, as well as the substance abuser, needs help. Substance abuse creates an imbalance in the relationship between the needs of the significant other and those of the substance abuser. Restoring some balance in the relationship is needed. Many significant others are prone to minimize their own problems and to believe these problems would disappear if the substance abuser simply got clean and sober. Experience teaches that this is not the case. The problems that result from being in a close relationship with a substance abuser tend to become ingrained and require attention in and of themselves.
- The second point is that, perhaps ironically, the best way to promote positive change in the substance abuser over the long run is for the significant other to assess and care for his or her own needs, thereby changing the dynamics of the substance abuser–codependent relationship in a fundamental way.

Significant others often build up considerable resentment toward the substance abusers. This comes in part from their frustrations in getting the substance abusers to stop drinking or using drugs and in part from the aforementioned imbalance in the relationship. As much as they may want to "let go" of the substance abusers and focus on their own needs, many significant others feel guilty doing so (i.e., they think that would be selfish), feel anxious about what would happen if they did so, or both. The therapist using the FRP needs to clearly and repeatedly challenge such thinking, emphasizing how caring detachment will prove to be the best course for both the user and the significant other in the long run. Here is a case example:

Tina had been married to Glenn for eight years. Throughout their marriage, he had abused heroin. He was employed as a health care professional, but due mainly to his substance abuse problem, he had failed three times to pass a certification exam that would have led to a substantial increase in salary. In addition, his drug habit had led them into a series of financial crises. Each time, Tina had been the one to work harder to bail them out.

Tina also had a sixteen-year-old sister, Marie, who had been living with her and Glenn for a year. Marie had moved in after her and Tina's mother had remarried and moved out of state, because she did not want to leave the high school she was in. Marie could be very oppositional and strong-willed, and like Glenn, she demanded a great deal of Tina's time and attention. She would not easily follow rules or help around the house. On the other hand, she was not shy about asking for money, the use of Tina's car, and so forth.

When first asked about herself, Tina just smiled and shrugged, as if to minimize the cumulative effects of the stress she was under as a result of Glenn's substance abuse problem and having to be a surrogate mother to a rebellious teenager. Through the assessment, however, the therapist learned Tina had been chronically tired for at least three years. Typically, she was in bed and asleep by 9 p.m. and had to be up by 5 a.m. to get ready for work herself and to rouse both Glenn and Marie. In the past two years, she missed more days from work on account of illness than she had missed in the previous ten years combined. She had lost any sexual desire a "long time ago." At one time committed to physical fitness, she couldn't remember the last time she had exercised regularly. And in the previous year, she had gained ten pounds.

Psychologically, spiritually, and emotionally, Tina was not well. Her self-esteem was very low, as manifested in frequent self-derogatory remarks, such as calling herself incompetent at being either a wife or a surrogate mother. She was clearly aware of being treated with a lack of respect and consideration but felt helpless to change her situation. In her mind, it was as though she was fated to be abused. Not surprisingly, she scored as moderately high on a standard measure of depression. She wasn't sure where her life was heading, and she felt hopeless and adrift. Tina's original motivation for seeking help reflected her despair: "I thought you might have some answers for me. I'm sure I'm doing something wrong, but I can't figure out what I should be doing instead."

Following the assessment, Tina's therapist took a few minutes to summarize how the stresses and frustrations of her relationships with Glenn and Marie had taken their toll on her. The therapist went on to suggest that part of what Tina might have to learn was how "less is more"—how taking better care of herself might, in fact, prove to be the best way to change things in her family. Tina had a hard time seeing this at first, but she agreed that because her way had not been working, she was willing to place her trust in the therapist for a while.

The summary, though brief, capitalized on information that Tina herself supplied. It proved to be influential in facilitating Tina's initial willingness to follow therapeutic recommendations. These recommendations were surprisingly simple, yet they turned out to be highly effective: Tina was encouraged to take two evenings a week—one to attend a Nar-Anon meeting and one to go to the health club where she had a long-neglected lifetime membership. She was encouraged and coached on how not to let anything interfere with her participation in these two activities. Lastly, she was not to prepare dinner in advance for Glenn and Marie on these evenings.

Her therapist predicted that Tina could expect to encounter resistance about being out two nights a week, in the form of discouragement and complaining from her husband and her sister, and the therapist prepared her for it. Tina was told that such resistance was to be expected as she took these first steps toward what the therapist called caring detachment. She and the counselor role-played these situations, and Tina was therefore prepared for them when they happened. Without this support—from both her therapist and the friends she was beginning to make at Nar-Anon—Tina said she doubted that she would have had the courage to persevere and probably would have given in and given up both Nar-Anon and the health club to stay home and take care of Glenn and Marie.

During one of her sessions, Tina described how her relationships with Glenn and Marie had started to change. Before she did this, however, she told her therapist how much better she was beginning to feel about herself. She lost five pounds and was beginning to recover some of her lost energy. She said that Glenn had been complaining a lot over the past month about her going to Nar-Anon meetings, which she increased to two per week. She told him that she found them very helpful and would not stop going. On at least two occasions, she said, she flatly refused to "lend" him money, knowing very well it would go for drugs and reported this exchange: "Last night he said to me, 'I want my old Tina back.' I actually laughed. I said, 'Well, this is the new Tina, so you might as well get used to her.'"

On the day before this interaction with Glenn, Marie had asked Tina if she could use her car to meet some friends. "Not tonight," Tina had replied, "it's my workout night." Marie frowned. At one time, she would have argued and maybe even cursed out Tina, but this time, she offered no back talk, for she knew somehow that Tina meant what she said. This little exchange marked a turning point in Tina's relationship with Marie.

This case illustrates how family recovery can begin with the recovery of one member. That member may not be the one with the substance use problem; on the contrary, it may be one of the psychologically healthiest members of the family. The change process begins when a significant other realizes that addiction has affected him or her and feels a need to start taking care of his or her own physical, emotional, and spiritual well-being. The family system begins to change as this person relates to himself or herself differently and, consequently, to others differently, as in the case of Tina.

Introducing Recovery Tasks

Before ending this initial session, the therapist should introduce the concept of recovery tasks and ask the client to follow through on two such initial tasks.

Recovery tasks consist of concrete suggestions made by the therapist that are intended to educate the codependent in key Twelve Step concepts, engage him or her in a collaborative relationship with the therapist, and facilitate the process of bonding to Al-Anon or Nar-Anon. Recovery tasks are given at the end of each session and followed up on at the outset of the next session.

For the assessment session, the therapist should begin by explaining that recovery tasks, although not required, are intended to promote clear thinking and to help the client decide how to redefine his or her relationship to the addict. Indicate that there will be no negative consequences if the client does not follow through on a particular recovery task; on the other hand, you will routinely follow up to see whether these tasks have raised any issues or questions. Explain that following through on recovery tasks will enhance the effectiveness of treatment by providing experiences that will make these treatment sessions more useful.

Explain that recovery tasks will typically include these four things:

1. Suggested Al-Anon or Nar-Anon meetings to attend
2. Suggested readings and handouts
3. Suggested things to do to feel more a part of Al-Anon or Nar-Anon
4. Suggestions for how to begin to detach in a caring way from the substance abuser

Explain that recovery tasks represent a collaboration between the client and yourself as the therapist. As an experienced professional, you will have some specific ideas for things the client could do between sessions in each of the areas mentioned. However, it is also important that the client become an active participant in the process of determining recovery tasks.

Readings

For this first session, give Topic 1: Handout 4, Reading Assignments, to your client. Review the handout, while asking the client to read chapter 1: "Bill's Story" and chapter 8: "To Wives" from *Alcoholics Anonymous* or chapter 1: "Who Is an Addict?" from *Narcotics Anonymous* or all three.[3] If the substance abuser uses only alcohol, then the reading from *Narcotics Anonymous* may be omitted. Explain that although these first readings are from AA and NA literature, future readings will also come from the book *Al-Anon Faces Alcoholism*.[4] Tell the client that you plan to discuss any reactions to these readings at the next session, and ask him or her to write down any reactions and thoughts in a journal if she or he has agreed to keep one.

Here are the recommended readings that appear in Topic 1: Handout 4:

> *Alcoholics Anonymous*, chapter 1: "Bill's Story" and chapter 8: "To Wives"[5]
>
> *Narcotics Anonymous*, chapter 1: "Who Is an Addict?"[6]

TREATMENT NOTE

Talking with Husbands about Chapter 8

Chapter 8 was written by the wife of a recovering alcoholic and was included in *Alcoholics Anonymous* as advice to spouses.[7] As such, it could easily have been titled "To Spouses." It is important to explain to male clients that it applies just as much to husbands as it does to wives, and the best time to do this is when the reading is assigned as a recovery task.

Deciding on Suggested Readings

The therapist will need to use his or her judgment when deciding whether to recommend readings from AA, NA, or both. Even when the user is solely a drug abuser, some readings from the AA Big Book, especially chapter 8, are still relevant. Also, readings from the text *Al-Anon Faces Alcoholism* are applicable regardless of the nature of the addiction, because the concepts of enabling and detaching are generic ones.[8]

Meetings

Because Al-Anon and Nar-Anon will be discussed in detail in session 2, the therapist may decide not to suggest that the client attend any Al-Anon or Nar-Anon meetings at this point unless the client has had some prior experience with Al-Anon or Nar-Anon, feels positively about that experience, and expresses a willingness to go to one or more meetings. The therapist should test this straightforwardly: Ask the client if she or he knows what Al-Anon or Nar-Anon is, if he or she has had any experience with either one of these fellowships, and if so, what that experience was like.

If the response to this inquiry is positive, the therapist can ask the client how she or he would feel about attending one or two Al-Anon or Nar-Anon meetings between sessions. If the client is open to this, give him or her a current Al-Anon or Nar-Anon meeting schedule (or both) and spend a few minutes identifying one meeting that would be convenient for the client to attend. Ask the client to write down any reactions to any meetings attended in his or her journal.

If the therapist detects ambivalence or a frankly negative reaction to this initial inquiry, defer any further discussion or recommendations about meetings until you have had a chance to discuss Al-Anon and Nar-Anon and explore these negative reactions more completely.

Journaling Handout

Before the session concludes, provide the client with Topic 1: Handout 5, Journaling Possibility: Reflections about Resentment and Shame, and explain that if he or she decides to keep a journal, he or she may want to consider exploring more deeply the subject of resentment and shame that were discussed in this session by answering the questions posed in the handout.

TREATMENT NOTE

Journaling

Journaling can be a useful method for enhancing the effectiveness of this intervention. For those clients who have prior experience in keeping a journal or diary, and those who are open to the idea, journaling is highly recommended. The therapist may wish to provide the client with a composition book for this purpose. Explain that you would like the client to use this journal to write down his or her thoughts about any of the recovery tasks she or he does, as well as any other significant thoughts or questions that occur between sessions. Explain that the journal is a private one that you will not read, but you will ask the client to talk about any journal entries she or he feels comfortable sharing at the beginning of each session.

Chapter 8 || Twelve Step Recovery

Topic 2: The Principles of Twelve Step Fellowships

In this session, the therapist reviews the client's reactions to the assessment process and initial recovery tasks, discusses with the client some basic assumptions shared by Twelve Step fellowships, and attempts to actively facilitate the client's initial involvement in Al-Anon or Nar-Anon or both.

Beginning with this session, all treatment sessions should follow this format: *review* of previous session, recovery tasks, and journal; presentation and discussion of new material; and discussion of new *recovery tasks*.

Review (10–15 Minutes)

Like most psychotherapists, the therapists who use this program will typically begin a session with a general inquiry into how the client's life has been going since the last session. Although appropriate, this checking-in process should not be permitted to grow into a lengthy digression that leaves little time left for the core material presented here. In addition, this initial phase of each FRP session is structured so that this initial inquiry is not freewheeling, but focused. Use of the session guidelines that accompany this book is recommended as an effective means of focusing each therapy session.

To underscore the importance of recovery tasks in this program, the therapist should be sure to begin the opening part of this and every subsequent session with a brief inquiry into the client's reactions to

- what was *discussed* in the last session,
- any *readings* that she or he did since the last session,
- any *meetings* that she or he attended,
- any *journal entries* or *handout responses* that she or he recalls and would like to share.

New Material (30 Minutes)

The facilitator should attempt to cover as much of the following material as possible. It is very important, however, to be sure to leave five minutes at the end of this (and every) session for the discussion of recovery tasks. Therefore, if all of the issues in the following list cannot be adequately covered with enough time left for recovery tasks, it is best to stop at some point, discuss recovery tasks, and continue the discussion of this topic at the next session. There is no reason a single topic must be covered in a single session.

In this session, the therapist seeks to engage the client in a frank and open-ended discussion of the following basic assumptions underlying the Twelve Step fellowships of AA, NA, Al-Anon, and Nar-Anon. These four fellowships all share a common view of addiction and recovery. The principles that guide them are described in their respective publications, but it is helpful to introduce them early on with the client in an organized way, in an effort to make certain that she or he has a basic understanding of them before going to a meeting.

An accurate understanding of Twelve Step fellowships and how they work can help alleviate anxieties and motivate the significant other to try Al-Anon or Nar-Anon and to enhance his or her ability to make optimum use of these fellowships. Conversely, to the extent that negative attitudes about AA, NA, Al-Anon, or Nar-Anon are based on misconceptions, false stereotypes, or prejudice, motivation to even give Al-Anon or Nar-Anon a try may be seriously undermined.

Begin by reading aloud the following excerpts from chapter 8 of *Alcoholics Anonymous* and ask the client to share his or her reactions. To facilitate the discussion, give the client Topic 2: Handout 1, Readings, which lists the following quotes. She or he may wish to answer the following questions in writing in more detail after the session:

> Our loyalty and the desire that our [spouses] hold up their heads and be like other [people] have [gotten us into] all sorts of predicaments. We have been unselfish and self-sacrificing. We have told innumerable lies to protect our

> pride and our [spouses'] reputations. We have prayed, we have begged, we have been patient. We have struck out viciously. We have run away. We have been hysterical. We have been terror stricken. . . . Our homes have been battlegrounds many an evening.[1]
>
> As animals on a treadmill, we have patiently and wearily climbed, falling back in exhaustion after each futile effort to reach solid ground.[2]

After reading these passages aloud, ask the *client* the following questions:

- Can you identify personally with any of these statements?
- In what ways has your relationship been like the one described in these passages?
- Do you ever feel frustrated or exhausted as a result of your loved one's substance use problem?

This kind of discussion provides a useful lead-in to the material that should now be presented.

Loss of Control

AA, NA, and other Twelve Step fellowships are founded on the notion that substance abuse progresses—from social use through habitual use to compulsive use. The problem drinker or drug user progressively loses control over his or her ability to limit substance use. The following passage from *Alcoholics Anonymous* captures the essence of loss of control:

> Here are some of the methods we have tried: Drinking beer only, limiting the number of drinks, never drinking alone, never drinking in the morning, drinking only at home, never having it in the house, never drinking during business hours, drinking only at parties, switching from scotch to brandy, drinking only natural wines, agreeing to resign if ever drunk on the job, taking a trip, . . .[3]

Narcotics Anonymous describes addiction in this way:

> Do we understand that we have no real control over drugs? Do we recognize that in the long run, we didn't use drugs—they used us? . . . Do we fully accept the fact that our every attempt to stop using or to control our using failed?[4]

The point in these statements is simple but clear: *Addiction implies loss of control, and loss of control means the progressive defeat of personal willpower.* As the substance abuser moves from being a Type One drinker or drug user to a Type Four drinker or drug user, as described in chapter 8 of *Alcoholics Anonymous*[5] she or he goes through an intense private struggle to limit or stop substance use. Despite occasional periods of sobriety, over the long run, the alcoholic or addict cannot reliably predict or control how much he or she will drink or use other drugs. As an AA saying has it, "No alcoholic wants *one* drink." Sooner or later, cravings overcome even the best of intentions, and the alcoholic or addict goes on a binge.

With each successive failure to control or limit use, self-esteem suffers more. The alcoholic or addict, unwilling to face the truth—that personal willpower is not working—either denies that the problem exists or else insists that she or he is still in control.

The First Step of AA as well as NA is a statement of acceptance of this loss of control over substance use. Taking this step is a major struggle for many substance abusers, who view it (correctly) as a defeat of individual willpower. Their denial reflects their unwillingness to face up to this simple yet stark reality: They cannot stop or effectively control substance use on their own.

Loss of control in substance abusers has its parallels in codependents. In fact, the First Step of Al-Anon is identical to the First Step of AA: "We admitted we were powerless over alcohol—that our lives had become unmanageable."[6] (The First Step in Nar-Anon is "We admitted we were powerless over the addict—that our lives have become unmanageable.")

Using the foregoing ideas as talking points, the therapist should engage the client in a discussion of loss of control in the substance abuser, using questions such as the following:

- In what ways has your loved one tried to limit or stop his or her substance use?
- Describe the loss-of-control process as you've observed it in your loved one.
- How has your loved one tried to avoid facing up to his or her powerlessness over alcohol or other drugs?

Next, apply the loss-of-control concept to the *client*, inquiring with questions such as these:

- Have you believed that you could somehow get your loved one to either reliably limit or stop substance use?
- Have you believed that your willpower alone could be enough to help your loved one overcome his or her substance use problem?
- Have you ever believed that if you just tried hard enough, you could get your loved one to stop substance use?
- Have you ever felt out of control or powerless when it came to your loved one's substance use?

Denial

Denial as a concept is nicely summarized in the description of the types of drinkers found in chapter 8 of *Alcoholics Anonymous*. Here are some excerpts:

> *Type One:* Your [spouse] may be only a heavy drinker. . . . It may be slowing him [her] up mentally and physically, but he [she] does not see it.
>
> *Type Two:* Your [spouse] is showing lack of control . . . He [she] often gets entirely out of hand when drinking. He [she] admits this is true, but is positive that he [she] will do better.
>
> *Type Three:* He [she] admits he [she] cannot drink like other people, but does not see why. He [she] clings to the notion that he [she] will yet find a way to do so.[7]

The same process applies, of course, to drug abuse. Denial is an integral part of addiction because it reflects the tendency, shared by most people in our culture, to resist accepting limitations on personal power. It has been suggested that our culture is heavily influenced by a social philosophy of *radical individualism*.[8] This ethic is based on a premise of extreme self-determination: We are the masters of our ships, the captains of our souls. As a result of this cultural bias, many men and women in our society are reluctant to accept the idea that they can be out of control of anything or the idea that they cannot overcome any problem through personal willpower alone. Such attitudes represent so-called rugged individualism in the extreme.

Although denial is a separate topic for a future session in the FRP, it is recommended that the therapist briefly test the waters now with regard to whether the client has a basic understanding of the concept, using questions such as the following:

- Can you relate to any of these quotations? In what ways has your loved one resisted facing up to the fact that she or he was losing control over substance use?
- Why do you think your loved one might not want to admit that she or he can't control substance use?

As in the earlier discussion of loss of control, apply the concept of denial also to the client, using questions such as these:

- How hard has it been for you to admit that your loved one was losing control over his or her substance use?
- Have you found yourself not wanting to admit that you cannot make your loved one stop using alcohol or drugs?

Spirituality and Fellowship versus Personal Willpower

If individual willpower alone cannot overcome addiction, then what can? Twelve Step fellowships such as AA, NA, Al-Anon, and Nar-Anon are based on the idea that alcoholism and other drug addictions can be overcome by turning to the resources of a Higher Power. This

Higher Power may be a Judeo-Christian conception of God, as it is for many, or it may be some other spiritual belief. Alternately, it may not be a concept of God at all. For example, the individual's "higher power" may be embodied in the fellowship of AA or NA itself. In other words, relying on group support and seeking the collective wisdom of the group is arguably a power greater than individual willpower.

Any or all of these can be construed as being stronger and wiser than the individual substance abuser struggling on his or her own to maintain control.

The therapist should introduce this idea of a power greater than individual willpower, elaborating on it by making the following three points:

First, although recovery for both the substance abuser and the significant other begins by admitting powerlessness over alcohol or drugs, this does *not* mean that either one is *helpless*. There is, in other words, an important difference between loss of control over substance use and helplessness to do anything about it. What AA and NA ask alcoholics and addicts to do as a First Step toward recovery is to give up any illusions they harbor that they can successfully control substance use and, instead, accept the need to give it up. Next, AA and NA ask those who want to stop drinking or using to reach out for help beyond themselves.

Similarly, what Al-Anon and Nar-Anon ask of significant others is to stop trying to control or protect the drinker or drug user. Substance abusers can do something about their substance abuse if they are willing to accept the problem and follow the program outlined in the Twelve Steps. But to the extent that significant others protect the substance abuser, the substance abuser will not be likely to face up to his or her powerlessness over substance use or be motivated to change.

The second point is that, on a spiritual level, both the substance abusers and their significant others must ultimately find the faith to believe that the problem of alcoholism or drug addiction can be overcome. This faith stands in opposition to the cynicism and despair that result from repeated failure to control or stop use without outside support. *Does the client have any hope at this point that his or her loved one's substance abuse problem can be overcome by reaching out to others?*

Third, on a practical level, AA, NA, Al-Anon, and Nar-Anon ask that we place ourselves in the hands of a fellowship and allow the collective wisdom of the group to guide our actions. This is of course a profound issue of trust that both substance abusers and their significant others must ultimately confront. *Is the client willing to trust others who have walked this path before enough to reserve judgment and follow their advice?*

Give the client Topic 2: Handout 2, Three Questions to Ask Yourself, and ask the client to share his or her reactions to each of the foregoing ideas. The client may write his or her responses in more detail after the session is over. It is not necessary to seek a heartfelt commitment to these concepts at this time, much less to try to change the client's beliefs. On the contrary, therapists should avoid taking any positions that could be perceived as proselytizing or criticizing. Rather, the objective here is to introduce these ideas and ascertain whether the client understands them in a basic way and how she or he reacts to them on a gut level. This dialogue will help the therapist to identify areas of potential resistance to basic Twelve Step concepts that may be the subject of future sessions.

TREATMENT NOTE

Discussing Higher Power

Introducing the concept of a Higher Power definitely does *not* mean that this subject should be allowed to turn into a protracted discussion, much less a debate, between the client and the therapist over their respective religious preferences or spiritual beliefs. This writer, for example, once supervised a therapist who quite seriously asked a client in their first session the following inappropriate question when introducing the concept of a Higher Power: "You don't have any problem with organized religion, do you?"

In approaching discussions about Higher Power, it helps if the therapist is reasonably clear in his or her own mind about his or her own spiritual beliefs and comfortable with them. Second, it is helpful if she or he is comfortable with divergent beliefs, including varied ways of thinking about God. With respect to Twelve Step fellowships and spirituality, the therapist must understand that by tradition, they are pluralistic, not dogmatic, in their interpretation of the concept of Higher Power. Bill Wilson, for example, stated: "You can, if you wish, make AA itself your 'higher power.' In this respect they are certainly a power greater than you, who have not even come close to a solution."[9]

What is primary at this time is not the client's particular views of God or his or her religiosity. What matters is that the client understands that AA and NA, and Al-Anon and Nar-Anon, challenge us to have hope that recovery can occur and also to place our trust in others who have struggled with similar issues before us. Collectively, these personal qualities—hope and trust—could be said to be an important part of our spirituality. The particular Higher Power that the substance abuser or the significant other chooses to place his or her faith in may be a traditional concept of God. Alternately, one's Higher Power may be the wisdom of a group conscience, which was described by Bill Wilson, cofounder of AA, in this way:

> We believe that every AA group has a conscience. It is the collective conscience of its own membership. Daily experience informs and instructs this conscience. . . . As this process continues, the group becomes better able to receive right direction for its own affairs. Trial and error produces group experience, and out of corrected experience comes custom. . . . The Greater Power is then working through a clear group conscience.[10]

What seems most apparent from both of the previous quotations is that substance abusers are challenged in AA and NA to abandon individual willpower in favor of the group and also, that Twelve Step fellowships have placed their faith in a kind of cultural evolution: the incremental development of a body of common wisdom and custom built on collective experience and community. This may well explain why some substance abusers report that going to AA or NA constituted their first experience of connectedness. The same applies to many significant others, who similarly describe Al-Anon and Nar-Anon as their "family."

Spiritual Renewal

Twelve Step fellowships recognize that addiction has progressively negative effects on self-esteem, faith, hope, and relationships. These are all facets of what we could call the *human spirit*. In Al-Anon and Nar-Anon, in particular, members are encouraged to pay attention to their own emotional, social, and spiritual needs; to focus less on the substance abusers in their lives; and to detach from efforts to control or protect the substance abusers. If the substance abuser is to change, Al-Anon and Nar-Anon believe that change is more likely to come indirectly—the result of the codependent's increasing detachment—than from efforts to directly control or shield the substance abuser.

Ask the client now to summarize in his or her own words how being in a relationship with a substance abuser has affected his or her own spirituality. As a guide, inquire briefly into each of these facets of spirituality:

- Self-esteem: Feelings of personal worth and competence, of what one has to offer to the world in general and one's value to others
- Faith: Belief in the meaningfulness of life and in a power greater than the self
- Hope: Optimism rather than pessimism, a belief that things can get better
- Relationships: Sense of connectedness to others, as opposed to alienation

To enhance reflection on this topic, give the client Topic 2: Handout 3, Spirituality, and suggest that later in the week the client write about his or her reactions to each of the four facets of spirituality: self-esteem, faith, hope, and relationships. The client may have additional reflections after the session is over.

Though hardly an inclusive definition of spirituality, the foregoing exercise can open a fruitful dialogue that raises issues that will prove relevant to the significant other's ability to bond to a fellowship. Again, this initial discussion need not be lengthy or exhaustive.

At this time, the therapist is checking to see that the client has a basic understanding of these ideas and is testing the client's gut reactions to them. Generally speaking, the more the individual's spirit has been wounded through addiction, the more reticent she or he will be to place faith in others again (and in a Higher Power).

Recovery Tasks (5 Minutes)

The following are suggested as recovery tasks for the codependent to be completed prior to the next FRP session:

Meetings

If this was not done at the end of the assessment session, now is the time to suggest to the client that she or he try going to one or two Al-Anon or Nar-Anon meetings (or both). The discussions just mentioned will, we hope, have been helpful in preparing the client for this suggestion. In addition, it is helpful if the therapist has on hand current Al-Anon and Nar-Anon meeting schedules covering the geographic area where the client lives.

If the client has had some prior exposure to Al-Anon or Nar-Anon and if this exposure was basically a positive experience, suggest that the client give it a try again now, this time using the relationship with the therapist as a vehicle for processing the new experience. *If you have one, give the client a current meeting schedule and help him or her identify a couple of meetings that would be convenient.* In many areas, current meeting schedules and brief descriptions of meetings are available online and can be easily printed out for use in FRP sessions. If the client is keeping a journal, ask that she or he also take a few minutes to write down reactions to any meetings attended. Remind the client that it is perfectly acceptable to just go and listen at meetings (i.e., they may choose not to talk much at first).

If the client appears resistant to the idea of going to Al-Anon or Nar-Anon, be sure to listen carefully to ascertain whether this reaction is based on actual experience at meetings or on stereotypes, prejudice, or misinformation about Twelve Step fellowships. If negative attitudes seem to be based on preconceived notions, as opposed to actual experience, it can be helpful to ask the client to share his or her image of Al-Anon and Nar-Anon: *What kinds of people do you imagine would go to an Al-Anon or Nar-Anon meeting, and what do you think happens there?* Engage the client in a discussion of his or her stereotypes and the expectations that arise from them. Stereotypes and prejudices can easily undermine a significant other's motivation to give a Twelve Step fellowship a try. Many times, these prejudices can be reduced if they are simply discussed openly.

Negative feelings based on actual experience often have their roots in unrealized expectations. Some people may have gone to one or more Al-Anon meetings hoping for quick solutions to their problem—as a way to get the alcoholic or addict in their lives to stop drinking or using drugs—only to be sorely disappointed when they discover a group of people who speak about detaching from the addict. Many people misconstrue detaching to mean rejection of the addict; not a few have said that they interpreted this talk to mean that they should divorce. Reluctant to ask questions, they never clarified their misconceptions. Feeling frustrated and disappointed, they ended up feeling worse after going to a meeting. "It made me feel depressed and hopeless to be with a group of people who seemed to be sitting in the same sinking boat as I was in, with no solution in sight," is what one significant other wrote in her journal after her first Al-Anon meeting.

Disappointment can also result when someone's initial exposure to Al-Anon or Nar-Anon is less than encouraging—for example, if members at a particular meeting share experiences that are considerably less than upbeat. Another significant other expressed dismay when she learned that some members at the Al-Anon meeting she attended had been going there for ten years. "I can't imagine doing that for ten years," she said. In response, the therapist pointed out that this woman's husband had already been an alcoholic for nearly *fifteen* years. Moreover, some significant others continue going to Al-Anon even after their loved one has become sober or after their relationship has ended, simply because they find it rewarding. This disappointed newcomer was advised to get to know not only this one group but several others much better before reaching a judgment about how helpful Al-Anon might be. By doing nothing different, the therapist said, the client could reasonably expect nothing to change for the better (i.e., the relational status quo would go on ad infinitum). On the other hand, by getting involved in Al-Anon now, even after fifteen years in an alcoholic marriage, and by starting to take care of her own emotional, social, and spiritual needs, she had good reason to hope that many things could change for the better in the future, both for herself and in her marriage. Detachment may take time, but it is ultimately productive for the loved ones of substance abusers, regardless of whether the substance abuser continues to drink or use.

A final example: The wife of an alcoholic went to her first Al-Anon meeting only to find that the group was small, that the members were much older than she was, and that they sat around a large table. She said that she tried to ignore these issues and concentrate instead on what was being said. But she left the meeting feeling unsatisfied. Her therapist reassured her that she could understand this reaction, saying the meeting sounded more formal than most. The therapist then pointed out that no two Al-Anon meetings are identical. "There is really no such thing as a 'standard' Al-Anon meeting," she said. "There are many different meetings, and each one varies depending on what the group wants. So maybe we need to scout out some different meetings for you to try out."

Were it not for frank discussions of their initial reactions to Al-Anon or Nar-Anon meetings, as illustrated by these examples, some significant others would not likely give Al-Anon and Nar-Anon a second try. In reaching hasty conclusions, they would have lost an opportunity for bonding and for the growth and renewal that fellowship offers.

Ask such clients to try to identify what it was they had expected from Al-Anon or Nar-Anon and why they were disappointed with their initial experiences. Again, open and honest discussion can help reduce resistance. The therapist's goal is not to challenge the client's prior experience; rather, it is to validate it and discuss it further. The therapist can be an effective problem-solver when the client's current resistance is understood in its proper context.

Having acknowledged and discussed any negative sentiments toward Al-Anon or Nar-Anon, the therapist should now try to enlist the client's cooperation in giving Al-Anon or Nar-Anon (or both) a try, either for the first time or again. Clients should be reassured that this time the therapist will be available and interested in their honest reactions to these experiences, with the goal of making the meetings helpful.

Remember to suggest to the client that she or he attend one or two Al-Anon or Nar-Anon meetings prior to the next session, and that she or he take a few moments to write down any reactions in her or his journal so that you can discuss it the next time you meet.

TREATMENT NOTE

Active Facilitation

If at any point in this facilitation program a client seems open to going to an Al-Anon or Nar-Anon meeting but seems anxious about doing so, it is appropriate to actively facilitate attendance. This is done by making a contact with an Al-Anon or Nar-Anon member who is willing to volunteer to talk to the client over the phone, to meet with him or her, to accompany him or her to a meeting, or any combination of these. This strategy can be very helpful in getting basically willing yet shy clients to attend their first meetings. It is also consistent with Step Twelve of the Twelve Step program. An Al-Anon or Nar-Anon volunteer appropriate for this task would be someone of the same sex as the client, who has been active in Al-Anon or Nar-Anon for at least a year, who has served as an Al-Anon or Nar-Anon sponsor, and who has a sponsor of his or her own. The facilitator may locate such volunteers by networking with local Al-Anon and Nar-Anon groups.

To implement active facilitation, the therapist should contact the Al-Anon or Nar-Anon volunteer by phone, preferably with the client present, and explain that the client would like to ask a few questions, talk to a "real" Al-Anon or Nar-Anon member, or have company at a first meeting. Then allow the client and the volunteer to talk together directly to make arrangements.

TREATMENT NOTE

Talking about the Substance Abuser

One issue that commonly arises in the course of this program that is best addressed from the outset is the tendency that many FRP clients will want to talk more or less exclusively about the substance abuser. This is, of course, understandable. It is often either the explicit or implicit agenda of significant others in seeking therapy in the first place to enlist a professional's help in their efforts to get their loved ones to stop drinking or drugging. "Tell me what I can do to get him or her to stop" is the not-so-hidden agenda of many clients. As such, they may persist in wanting to talk about how to change the alcoholic or addict, whereas the facilitator's goal is to talk about how *they* (i.e., the significant others) can change.

From the Al-Anon perspective, the answer to the client's question may seem like a paradoxical (and confusing) one. The main tenet of Al-Anon is that the codependent needs to learn to detach from the alcoholic's substance use: to let go of the alcoholic, to change his or her own behavior and way of relating to the alcoholic, and to focus on his or her own needs and development. He or she is urged to detach: to stop protecting the abuser from the natural consequences of his or her substance abuse, to stop trying to substitute his or her own willpower for that of the alcoholic, and thereby to alter the status quo in the relationship.

Because they are not accustomed to this point of view, many significant others may persist in wanting to discuss their partners' substance use from a naïve problem-solving perspective: "Tell me what I can do to get him or her to stop." Many may initially perceive the facilitator's and Al-Anon's message—in effect, that "less is more"—as unsatisfying. They may express disappointment and frustration. The therapeutic challenge is to show sympathy for the client's distress—indeed, his or her plight—while at the same time steering him or her progressively away from an enabling relationship with the substance abuser toward caring detachment. Concretely, this means allowing the client to vent his or her frustrations yet consistently resisting any temptation to allow the session to digress to an endless discussion of the substance abuser and what she or he is doing. Such digression would not leave enough time for discussion of the significant other and what he or she needs to do to alter the way she or he relates to the substance abuser.

Readings

Give your client Topic 2: Handout 4, Reading Assignments. Review the handout, while asking the client if she or he would be willing to read the material prior to the next session. Include readings from *Narcotics Anonymous* and the NA pamphlet only if the client is in a relationship with a drug abuser.[11] Readings for this session include

Alcoholics Anonymous, chapter 2: "There Is a Solution" and chapter 3: "More About Alcoholism"[12]

Al-Anon Faces Alcoholism, pages 91–103: "Serenity Does Not Depend on Sobriety," "Living with Al-Anon, We Learn to Live," "Perfectly Good People Get Alcoholism: A Professional Looks at Her Attitudes," and "The Face of an Angel"[13]

Narcotics Anonymous, chapter 2: "What Is the Narcotics Anonymous Program?" and chapter 3: "Why Are We Here?"[14]

NA pamphlet *Am I an Addict?* (www.na.org/?ID=ips-eng-index)[15]

Caring Detachment

Beginning with this session, the facilitator should end each session with one or two specific suggestions as to what the client can do to begin to decrease his or her enabling relationship with the substance abuser and move instead toward caring detachment. This process needs to be a collaborative one. As discussed earlier, detachment and enabling cannot always be rigidly defined, as in labeling actions as *this* behavior is caring detachment or *that* is enabling. What may constitute detachment in one relationship may actually seem more like enabling in another. A major factor to consider is what has been the status quo in the relationship.

The therapist needs to begin, then, by developing a clear sense of the existing dynamics of the substance abuser–codependent relationship. A good question to ask yourself is this: How does the codependent usually react to the substance abuser, and what kind of behavioral change in the codependent would represent a change in that dynamic? Another way to put it is this: How could the client change the way she or he relates to the substance abuser so that the client is being honest, takes better care of him or herself, and allows the substance abuser to be more responsible?

Detachment is not an all-or-nothing sort of approach. There are degrees of caring detachment, and changing the substance abuser–codependent relationship is a goal that sometimes is best approached incrementally. Positive experiences in early attempts to detach, coupled with support from the therapist and from Al-Anon or Nar-Anon, can reinforce change in the significant other. The reinforcement for change comes when the client sees that she or he is taking better care of his or her mental, physical, spiritual, or social health, or combinations of these and as the substance abuser reacts to these changes. It is therefore very important that the therapist point out such changes in the client's behavior, as well as the reactions of the substance abuser, as a way of supporting caring detachment.

The following case example is intended to illustrate how detaching can be initially approached.

Janet said this to her counselor in their first session: "I'm not coping well. I'm furious on a regular basis. I get a headache about every other day, and I don't sleep well, so I'm chronically tired." Janet was angry at her husband, Tony, an alcoholic and cocaine addict whose license had been suspended after a second DWI arrest, because she had developed a pattern of consistently giving things up that were important to her in order to take care of him. For example, she was scheduled for a physical exam, but when Tony asked her to drive him to a job interview, she said yes. He was late getting out from the interview, and as a result, she missed her appointment. "These things happen all the time," she complained.

In the assessment, Janet had identified Tony's stage of substance abuse, using the relational model presented earlier, as Stage Four: "He's a slave," she said, "and alcohol and other drugs are his master." She also identified with the deep resentment and alienation commonly experienced by significant others at that stage, commenting, "I walk around feeling resentful all the time, and I just know that can't be good for my emotional or physical health."

As evidence to support her opinion that her husband was indeed a compulsive user, Janet cited the following facts: he had lost his license for six months as a result of the second DWI arrest, he had lost two consecutive jobs due to excessive absenteeism, he had stolen money from Janet and from his parents, and he had become a chronic liar. Despite these consequences, he continued to drink and get high, lamely arguing that he had cut back. "And he lies so much to cover his tracks," Janet said, "that he's gotten in the habit of lying about things he doesn't even have to lie about."

In her relationship with Tony, Janet was not only chronically angry but terribly confused:

> I really don't know what to do. Sometimes, I think I should refuse to help him out at all, but on the other hand, I want things to get better. That's why I took him for that interview, even though I know very well that he's still using and probably wouldn't last more than a couple of weeks on the job if he got it. Also, I don't know what to talk to him about anymore, and what not to talk about. I mean, do I vent my anger every time I feel it? If I did that, I'd be yelling at him every day. On the other hand, if I keep my lip buttoned, I just walk around steaming.

Janet's situation was not atypical of loved ones when they first seek help. They want to know what to do to change the addict, though Al-Anon teaches that what they really need help with is how to change themselves. The therapist who uses this program will no doubt encounter Janet's sentiments and her situation time and time again. The challenge is to reassure the client that Al-Anon and the counselor have an idea of how the client's life can change for the better and how that change could influence the substance abuser in a positive way. However, that change may not be what the significant other expected.

Janet was prepared by her counselor for the reality that Tony might not welcome changes in her. In fact, the counselor said, Tony might even try to undermine any changes that Janet attempted to make in the way she related to him. "He is used to a status quo," the counselor said, "and when you change yourself and the way you relate to him, even in small ways, that will signal a change in the status quo, and you can expect a reaction."

With this in mind, Janet and the counselor jointly decided that a good place to begin the process of detachment was for Janet to do two things: (1) let Tony know that she started seeing a counselor because she wanted to work on how his substance abuse had affected her and (2) tell Tony that she was going to have her paycheck deposited automatically into a separate checking account in her name only. That way, he could not steal money by making withdrawals from a joint account without telling her, and she would be assured of having at least enough money to pay the essential household bills.

The counselor specifically advised Janet not to allow herself to get into arguments with Tony over these decisions or to attempt to provoke a reaction from him by presenting them in a hostile way. Instead, she was told to simply state them straightforwardly as decisions she made for herself (because money had become a big stressor in her life). She and the counselor role-played some potential interactions Janet might have with Tony, including him accusing her of punishing him or of trying to control him. Janet, of course, knew her husband best, and she could predict that these would, in fact, be likely reactions. She was right. Tony became furious and at one point stormed out of the house, only to return an hour later because he had neither money nor a vehicle.

One outcome of this case was that Tony ended up entering a treatment program about four months after Janet started seeing the counselor. That was a highly gratifying outcome for Janet. Just as important, however, was the fact that at the end of that time, she no longer found herself experiencing the stress of chronic resentment, she was no longer feeling chronically tired, her headaches had gone away, and the couple's finances were in much better shape. Through Al-Anon, Janet had made the first new friends she had had in years. She started a regular program of exercise and was, in general, happier than she had been, in her estimation, in two decades. She was hopeful that Tony would recover from his addictions, but she was equally determined to maintain the changes in her own lifestyle even if he didn't.

Chapter 9 || A Closer Look at Al-Anon and Nar-Anon

Topic 3: Al-Anon and Nar-Anon

The goal of this session is to extend the discussion of Al-Anon and Nar-Anon, with particular attention to their key traditions and the resources these fellowships have to offer. As with other sessions, however, it begins with a review of the client's experiences since the last session, with special emphasis on his or her reactions to recovery tasks.

Review (10–15 Minutes)

The therapist should be sure to inquire specifically about each of the following:

Journal and Handouts

Did the client start a journal or respond to anything contained in the handouts? If so, are there any entries that she or he would like you to read (or would like to read to you)? Take a few minutes to discuss any such journal entries or responses, and encourage the client to continue writing.

Readings

Did the client follow up on any of the suggested readings from *Alcoholics Anonymous*, *Narcotics Anonymous*, or *Al-Anon Faces Alcoholism*?[1] If so, what reactions did she or he have? Were you able to give the client the NA pamphlet *Am I an Addict?*, and if so, did he or she read it?[2]

Based on initial readings, plus the discussion of stages of use in session 1, at what stage in the addiction process does the significant other believe the substance abuser to be in at this time?

Take a moment to inquire about the client's reaction to the idea, also raised in the last session, of being powerless to stop a problem drinker or drug user from substance use. How does that idea sit with him or her now that there has been some time to think about it? Is he or she really accepting of it, or does some part of the person resist that idea? Explain that this is an important question—one that is worthy of careful thought and discussion—because it relates directly to the First Step of AA and Al-Anon.

Many loved ones of substance abusers secretly cling to a belief that it's possible to get a substance abuser clean and sober, if you just try hard enough. This belief almost inevitably leads to a preoccupation with the substance abuse and to enabling. On the other hand, if we truly accept the idea that we cannot make someone else's decisions for her or him—including a substance abuser's decision about getting sober—then we are free to allow her or him to be responsible for themselves (including dealing with any negative consequences associated with substance abuse), which opens the way to caring detachment.

Next, introduce the idea of the client starting to shift attention away from the addict, toward his or her own needs. This shifting of focus also facilitates caring detachment. It is an idea that is much easier to act on if one first accepts the notion that we are unable to change anyone other than ourselves. The story titled "The Face of an Angel" in *Al-Anon Faces Alcoholism* expresses this idea in a clear and poignant way.[3] The therapist can ask the significant other if she or he has read this story. If not, the therapist may want to summarize it and then discuss the basic idea of detaching that this story so aptly presents.

Meetings

Inquire next about any reactions to Al-Anon or Nar-Anon meetings that the client may have attended. Because these may be a significant other's first exposure to Twelve Step fellowships, take some extra time in this session to elicit and explore reactions to these first meetings, with special attention to resolving issues that might undermine a client's motivation for attending future meetings. Common forms of resistance include a reluctance to identify with other members, discomfort with spirituality, social shyness, and last but not least, saying: "I'm not as bad off as those people!" This last form of resistance can be handled by pointing out that Al-Anon and Nar-Anon can be as helpful for concerned others of those with more moderate substance abuse problems as they are for concerned others of those with severe addictions.

Caring Detachment

Did the client make any initial efforts at practicing caring detachment? If so, what did he or she do? Does what he or she say strike the therapist as movement toward caring detachment? Especially in these early sessions, it is important not only to encourage and reinforce caring detachment but also to be sure the significant other understands the concept and is acting consistently with it in relation to the substance abuser. Consider the following example of one client who confused detaching with *accommodating*.

Julie had lived with her boyfriend Jake for three years. She first noticed that he had a drinking problem after they moved in together. She had always known that he liked to drink, but while they were dating, she didn't realize that he drank not only when they went out, but all the time. Weekdays, he would often start with a beer in the morning before going to work and then stop at a bar for two or three more on the way home. He admitted to Julie that the only reason he didn't drink on the job was that he worked in construction and would have been fired on the spot if his supervisor caught him with a beer. Evenings and weekends, he drank more or less continuously. He was rarely farther than an arm's length from a beer.

Although they fought occasionally about paying bills (Jake spent too much in the bar and often came up short when it was time to pay his share of the household expenses), so far the negative consequences associated with his drinking had been largely interpersonal: Julie's feelings for Jake had started to change. As she put it, she still loved him, but she was definitely no longer as attracted to him as she once had been. She felt that this change in her was directly related to how she felt about his drinking. In turn, it was beginning to cause trouble between them. For example, Julie found that she did not want to make love with Jake anymore when he smelled of beer. And day-to-day life had become quite boring for her, with him usually falling asleep on the couch by nine at night.

In time, Julie found herself making little sarcastic comments about Jake's drinking, particularly about his after-work "shopping trips" to the bar and his early bedtime. He acted as though he didn't hear these comments. In time, she started making more pointed remarks. To these, he responded with irritation, calling Julie "Mother." So far, she avoided confronting Jake with her most serious concern about his drinking, though, which had to do with her changing feelings toward him.

Julie decided to get some counseling for herself after one more bridge had been crossed. It had been her most difficult interaction with Jake to date. He had approached her for sex one night, and she said something about his being too drunk. He exploded. He stormed out of their apartment and did not show up until the next evening, refusing to tell Julie where he had been. In response to his demands, she found herself apologizing, though only halfheartedly, and internally, it bothered her a great deal to do so.

After meeting with the counselor, Julie thought she understood what detachment was all about. At the start of the next session, she said that things were much better between her and Jake. The counselor asked why—what had changed? Julie explained that she decided to stop talking to Jake about his drinking and, in her words, "To just see where things go between us." The counselor was puzzled. She asked Julie if that meant Jake's drinking didn't bother her anymore. Julie shook her head. "Oh, it still bothers me, all right, but talking to him about it just leads to a fight. So I decided to keep my feelings to myself."

To this the counselor replied, "To tell you the truth, what you're describing sounds to me more like enabling than detaching. You're giving Jake a signal that the status quo in your relationship is fine, when it isn't. From my point of view, you started to detach that night you told him the truth about how his drinking affects your sexual desire. That was a signal that things were not okay. Actually, you were taking care of yourself by being honest and not compromising your sexuality. You weren't just complaining—you were confronting him with a reality. You were also allowing Jake to experience the natural—and perfectly understandable—consequences of his drinking, which is your loss of attraction. How will you feel having sex with Jake when he smells of beer?"

This discussion proved to be very productive. Julie began to be honest again with Jake. She extended this beyond her sexual feelings and told him about how she was bored with the rut their life was in. She started making dates to see old friends with whom she had fallen out of touch, and she also started going to Al-Anon. The tension in her relationship with Jake did increase, but he also started drinking less. A few months later, she told him that she was no longer sure that she wanted to commit to Jake and had decided they should live apart. At that point, he said he would go for help about his drinking. Julie replied that that was probably a good idea for Jake. "I told him I really hope it works out for him because I care about him, and I think that eventually, drinking the way he does will kill him." She told him she still had some hope that their relationship would work out. "But for now," she said, "I told him I preferred to be on my own."

New Material

In this session, the therapist should endeavor to engage the significant other in a discussion of some of the key traditions that guide the fellowships of Al-Anon and Nar-Anon and also help the significant other identify some of the resources that Al-Anon and Nar-Anon have to offer in support of his or her own recovery.

Al-Anon and Nar-Anon and the Importance of Community

To begin this discussion of Al-Anon and Nar-Anon Traditions, point out that the Twelve Steps all use the word *we* instead of *I*. This is because all Twelve Step fellowships are founded on the belief that group support is superior to individual willpower when it comes to stopping alcohol or other drug abuse. Al-Anon and Nar-Anon believe that individuals who have loved ones who have substance use problems can effectively learn to cope with those substance use problems by opening themselves up to and availing themselves of that mutual support. Beyond that, Al-Anon and Nar-Anon are based on the belief that the substance abuser is more likely to pursue recovery when his or her loved ones stop enabling the substance abuse problem. Here is an example:

Lisa had been married to Jeff for five years. They had two young children, ages four and two. Jeff was a habitual drinker and a frequent user of cocaine, and his habits were creating a major financial crisis for the family. Lisa saw a counselor who urged her to begin attending Al-Anon or Nar-Anon meetings in her area. She found Al-Anon more accessible and also felt more comfortable at Al-Anon because her own father had been an alcoholic. She learned, both through counseling and at those first Al-Anon meetings, that she had been enabling Jeff's use by taking responsibility for managing their increasingly difficult finances. She concluded that this approach was only forestalling disaster. In addition, it was causing her to feel continually anxious, to the point that she was waking up three or four times a night. When she asked her personal physician to prescribe a sleep aid, the physician did, but she also recommended that Lisa seek counseling.

Lisa began to detach first by speaking up about their financial problems. She had hesitated to do so only because she felt it would make no difference. "If it gets a reaction," one woman at a meeting said, "then that's a difference. You take that and you go from there." Her counselor agreed, adding only the caveat that Lisa was better off bringing these things up when Jeff was sober.

Lisa had never been an assertive type, so she needed a lot of support from the other members of Al-Anon to experiment with changes in the way she related to Jeff. He sensed this and began to complain about her going to meetings, saying it sounded like "a bunch of man haters." But Lisa persisted. Next she spoke to Jeff about her concerns about him as a role model for their children, especially in light of her experiences with her alcoholic father. She felt that her remote and unsatisfying relationship with her father was a major reason she had grown up with poor self-esteem.

A crisis point in the marriage came when Lisa, who worked full time, like Jeff, but actually made more money than he did, refused to give him $50 when he asked for it, saying she needed the money for bills. Jeff took her purse, emptied the contents onto the floor, and then took all the cash from her wallet. Lisa e-mailed two of her Al-Anon friends to tell them about this incident, and that night she shared it at an Al-Anon meeting. Over the next several days, she received e-mails and text messages daily from at least two other members offering support and asking her how she was doing. This made a big difference for Lisa, who told her counselor she probably could not have done what she was doing if it weren't for the support she was getting from her Al-Anon friends. She knew that she needed to have the courage to persevere, and she knew that the community of Al-Anon would be there for her.

Ask the client to share his or her reactions to this idea that fellowship and group support can be superior to going it alone when learning to detach from another person's substance use problem. Questions such as the following can help facilitate this discussion. (You may want to give the client Topic 3: Handout 1, Four Questions to Ask Yourself, which lists the following questions.) The client may wish to answer them in writing in more detail after the session:

- Have you ever felt all alone in your struggle to deal with ____________'s substance abuse problem?
- Have you ever felt overwhelmed, helpless, or hopeless in the face of ___________'s substance abuse problem?
- Have you hesitated to reach out to others for support and guidance in dealing with ____________'s substance use problem? If so, why?
- Have you been afraid to express your true feelings to ____________ about his or her substance use? Why?

Spirituality

Spirituality is another strong tradition within Twelve Step fellowships. Like AA and NA, Al-Anon and Nar-Anon, espouse faith in a Higher Power. Many individuals misinterpret this as a statement of religious orthodoxy when, in fact, it is not that at all. Rather, the approach to faith advocated by Twelve Step fellowships has been described as follows:

> Faith [in the Twelve Step sense] refers to the personal actions and responses involved in awakening to meanings and values, and in committing the self to centers of value, images, and reality of power, and in core stories that link persons to others who share them.[4]

It is in this sense that AA and NA call themselves programs of spiritual renewal. Bill Wilson, for example, described AA as a fellowship that was founded on the idea that an excessive belief in personal willpower constitutes an ultimately self-destructive core story by which to live. He wrote:

> The first requirement is that we be convinced that any life run on self-will can hardly be a success. . . . Most people try to live by self-propulsion. Each person is like an actor who wants to run the whole show; is forever trying to arrange the lights, the ballet, the scenery and the rest of the players in his own way. If his arrangements would only stay put, if only people would do as he wished, the show would be great.[5]

This is one way of saying that a culture that embraces a social philosophy of radical individualism, thereby promoting self-reliance to an extreme, is spiritually dysfunctional. No one can truly be such an island unto themselves. As a society, we set ourselves up for personal and relational dysfunction on a massive scale when we create a cult of self-reliance. Conversely, it has been argued that there is power to be derived from acknowledging personal limitation.[6] That power has its roots in humility and willingness to trust the collective wisdom of a group of concerned individuals and to follow its advice.

The spirituality of Twelve Step fellowships is based on the concept that group bonding and collective wisdom is superior to radical individualism as an approach to life. Group members seek collective strength by humbly accepting individual limitation. They have a set of shared values as expressed in the Twelve Steps, in the Serenity Prayer,[7] and in their Traditions. They seek to foster interpersonal connectedness and reliance on group support and on wisdom passed down, as opposed to self-will run riot. They seek to promote growth and renewal through advocacy of a core story that challenges the idea that we are all islands unto ourselves and that emphasizes instead acceptance of personal limitation and surrender to a power greater than personal ego.

This brief overview is intended to clarify the difference between a *fellowship* that is guided by what could be called a spiritual philosophy and a rich oral history and an *organized religion*, which neither AA nor Al-Anon (nor any other Twelve Step fellowship) is. There is no priesthood, secular or otherwise, to be found in Twelve Step fellowships. There is only the most loosely organized central organization, which bears no responsibility for issuing, monitoring, or correcting dogma. This is very important for the significant other to understand: *Twelve Step fellowships advocate an approach to life and a system of values, but not a particular concept of God, much less a religious dogma.*

Even if the client has not expressed concerns or reservations about religiosity and its place in Al-Anon or Nar-Anon, the therapist is wise to raise this issue anyway. Ask the client if she or he experiences any discomfort about the idea of a Higher Power as it is used in Twelve Step fellowships and if so, why. Listen carefully to any concerns or objections and then try to clarify them in light of the preceding information. Point out that the client is not likely to encounter protracted discussions of religion at Al-Anon or Nar-Anon meetings, though there may be some talk about spirituality. In Al-Anon and Nar-Anon, individuals are free to interpret the concept of a Higher Power in any way they choose, so long as they acknowledge some power or force greater and wiser than sheer individual willpower.

Fellowship with Alcoholics Anonymous and Narcotics Anonymous

Al-Anon and Nar-Anon, by tradition, stand as fellowships of peers that are independent of AA and NA, but that, nevertheless, remain committed to AA and NA and the Twelve Step program as an effective way for individuals to overcome problems with alcohol or drugs. Significant others should be made aware of the faith that Al-Anon and Nar-Anon place in AA and NA. Rather than trying to reform or cure a partner's substance use problem, Al-Anon and Nar-Anon members encourage one another to detach. If and when the substance abuser wants help to stop drinking or using drugs, he or she can be referred to the resources of AA or NA or both. It is not the significant other's responsibility to monitor, much less coordinate, the substance abuser's recovery.

The therapist should check to see that the client understands this concept of fellowship with AA and NA and how Twelve Step fellowships work together based on common values and ideas about the nature of addiction and recovery.

Resources: How Al-Anon and Nar-Anon Help

The point has been made that to the uninitiated, Al-Anon and Nar-Anon (like AA and NA) are often mistaken for religious organizations. In reality, they are fellowships (or extended families of sorts) that provide an array of resources for the support and welfare of their members. The therapist should reiterate this point and take some time to describe the following resources that Al-Anon and Nar-Anon offer.

Information Services

Telephone numbers for Al-Anon and Nar-Anon information services can be found in many local telephone books. Increasingly, Twelve Step fellowships have websites that include downloadable resources (pamphlets, etc.) and current meeting schedules. Telephone numbers are listed in the white pages under "Al-Anon (or Nar-Anon) Family Groups." If Al-Anon or Nar-Anon are not listed, individuals can try calling or searching InfoLine (211 in most states or www.infoline.org on the Web) or similar public information services. These services will often have current meeting schedules. In addition, both Al-Anon and Nar-Anon can be found online by simply typing in their names to any popular search engine.

Services such as InfoLine may sometimes refer callers to crisis counseling services. Staffed by trained nonprofessionals, these services offer comfort, support, and basic advice to callers who have acute needs. In general, the advice offered by these crisis services is consistent with Twelve Step philosophy and will be simple and practical. Most often the caller will be urged to get to a meeting as soon as possible to get face-to-face support in dealing with his or her situation.

TREATMENT NOTE

Making Calls for Substance Abusers

The therapist may want to let clients know that substance abusers can also make use of these referral services if and when they are ready to seek help for their alcohol or drug problem. The client may want to make this information available to the substance abuser; however, the significant other should not be the one to get information (i.e., make the calls) for the substance abuser, because to do so would only serve to reinforce the idea that the client is responsible for the substance abuser's recovery. From the outset, it is the substance abuser who should take responsibility (and therefore get the credit) for his or her decision to pursue recovery.

The Importance of Meetings

Meetings, of course, are the heart of all Twelve Step fellowships. Al-Anon and Nar-Anon are self-supporting fellowships that charge no user fees. Significant others should be aware that anyone attending an Al-Anon or Nar-Anon meeting may contribute a small amount to pay for items such as coffee or publications that the group lends to members. However, there is no obligation to contribute any money; therefore, lack of money represents no barrier to taking advantage of Al-Anon or Nar-Anon.

Meetings are open to anyone who has a family member or loved one who has an alcohol or other drug problem. The focus of meetings, however, is often at least as much on the welfare and growth of those who are there as it is on the substance abusers with whom they are in relationships. Initially, this focus on the loved ones of substance abusers instead of on the substance abusers may frustrate or disappoint the newcomer, especially one who is feeling desperate and seeks an immediate solution to how to get the drinker or drug user to stop. Sometimes, codependents go to their first meetings hoping to hear something new. In time, it is hoped, they come to see the usefulness of focusing on their own growth and on changing the basic structure and dynamics of their relationships with the substance abusers as the wiser path than trying to substitute their own willpower and motivation for substance abusers' behaviors or trying to control substance users through some single act or intervention on their parts.

Meetings offer social contact and friendship, a supportive environment in which to vent emotions, practical advice on handling difficult situations, suggestions for how to detach instead of enabling the addict, and in general, the opportunity to learn from others' stories of recovery. One of the keys to Al-Anon and Nar-Anon's effectiveness lies in the abilities of members to identify with and learn from each others' experiences and to support each others' efforts to change their relationships with the substance abusers.

The therapist might want to take a few moments here to solicit questions about meetings and provide additional information about Al-Anon or Nar-Anon. To the extent that the therapist is personally familiar with any Al-Anon or Nar-Anon meetings, she or he can share information that might encourage the reluctant client to get to his or her first meeting.

Publications

Al-Anon and Nar-Anon publish a number of books and pamphlets, including the book *Al-Anon Faces Alcoholism* that is used as a basic text in this FRP.[8] Books and pamphlets, which are often available through group meetings, not only explain Al-Anon and Nar-Anon concepts but can also augment and help clarify what the client hears at meetings. Clients should be encouraged to use Al-Anon and Nar-Anon publications in this way, because they serve as a source of comfort and advice between meetings.

Telephone Therapy

The therapist should advise clients in advance that some people at Al-Anon and Nar-Anon meetings will likely ask to exchange phone numbers (and, these days, e-mail addresses). To some newcomers—especially those who are socially shy or ambivalent about Al-Anon or Nar-Anon—this can be a discomforting experience at first. Some individuals misinterpret these efforts to reach out as efforts to establish a level of intimacy they find uncomfortable.

Explain to clients that people like themselves have found that as addiction progresses, many significant others find themselves becoming increasingly isolated from their own support networks of family and friends. This may be a consequence of wanting to avoid the shame and stigma they fear would result if their loved ones' substance problems became known. In time, this social avoidance and secrecy can evolve into a *wall of silence* that surrounds the significant other. Breaking through this wall—for instance, by opening oneself to contact with other Al-Anon or Nar-Anon members—can be no easy task, especially if the isolation has been long-standing. Therapists may find themselves working very hard with the loved ones of substance abusers on this basic issue of becoming open to support and contact. However, it can be immensely rewarding—even lifesaving, according to many Al-Anon and Nar-Anon members.

Explain to the client that the use of "telephone (and e-mail) therapy" is a long-standing tradition and a vital part of the Twelve Step recovery culture. Al-Anon, Nar-Anon, AA, and NA members are all encouraged to call other members for support not only in times of crisis but also to relieve the sense of isolation and chronic frustration that many of them must live with day to day. To use the telephone and Internet effectively, however, one must first overcome any anxiety or ambivalence that may stand in the way.

Aside from breaking through the social isolation that many loved ones of substance abusers experience, maintaining contact with other Al-Anon or Nar-Anon members has a practical purpose having to do with crises. One therapist who used the FRP would routinely ask the following question when discussing telephone and e-mail therapy: "When you're in a jam, who would you rather contact: a stranger or a friend?" The answer is obvious. Significant others need to develop a network of Al-Anon or Nar-Anon friends *in advance of a crisis* to feel comfortable using that network if and when a crisis does occur. This is an important reason for getting and using other members' phone numbers and e-mail addresses, and in general for getting to know others through meetings.

Sponsors

Although more will be said about sponsors in later FRP sessions, the therapist should at least briefly discuss this important resource in the present context of introducing the client to Al-Anon and Nar-Anon.

Ask the client if she or he has heard this term and, if so, what his or her idea of a sponsor is. Check to see that the client is aware of these basic points: A sponsor is an active member of Al-Anon or Nar-Anon who takes on a responsibility something like that of a coach. A sponsor is chosen voluntarily and should be of the same sex as the client. A sponsor should have been active in Al-Anon or Nar-Anon for at least two years and should have a sponsor of his or her own.

For the newcomer, a sponsor is a source of information about Al-Anon or Nar-Anon and about "working" the Twelve Step program, in addition to being an important source of comfort, support, and advice. A sponsor is not a therapist or a marriage counselor, however; nor should a sponsor be thought of as someone who has the last word on any issue. Sponsors can be changed at any time and probably should be changed once in a while.

Newcomers can benefit a great deal from establishing a relationship with a temporary sponsor for their first six months in the fellowship. Regular one-to-one contact with a sponsor affords an opportunity to ask questions and to share feelings that the newcomer might be reluctant to ask or share in a group. Many misconceptions about the Twelve Step program and about Al-Anon or Nar-Anon can be corrected through the sponsor-newcomer relationship, and the process of bonding to the fellowship can also begin through this relationship.

To get a sponsor, a newcomer needs only to state at the start of one or more meetings that she or he is looking for a temporary sponsor. Members who qualify and who feel ready to take on this role will identify themselves. It is advisable that newcomers talk with potential sponsors (preferably two or more potential sponsors) several times before reaching a mutual agreement to establish a sponsor-sponsee relationship.

Summing Up

Before moving on to recovery tasks, take a moment to ask the client to share what she or he got out of this session. What did she or he learn? What, if anything, was valuable about this session? Does she or he have any questions about the things that were discussed? Simply repeat the two or three points you especially wanted to stress this session, and check to see that those points have been received.

Recovery Tasks

The suggested recovery tasks to follow up on this topic are as follows:

Meetings

The therapist should again make a specific suggestion that the client attend two Al-Anon or Nar-Anon meetings before the next session. Again, it is advisable to have on hand current Al-Anon and Nar-Anon meeting schedules for use in locating meetings that would be convenient in terms of time and location.

If the client has not yet gone to any meetings but now expresses a willingness to do so, identify two meetings that would be convenient. Remind the client to identify himself or herself as a newcomer and to focus primarily on listening at these initial meetings. She or he should listen with the goal of trying to identify with at least some of what is said. Also, encourage the client to comment on these first experiences at meetings in his or her journal.

Newcomers need to be made aware that they will likely find meetings differ from one another. Explain that this is one reason you are suggesting they attend two different meetings. Also, advise clients that they may not relate to everyone at a meeting but that if they listen with an open mind, they may well be able to identify with at least some aspects of many members' experiences.

TREATMENT NOTE

Approaching Resistance

When dealing with reluctant or skeptical clients, one initial strategy is to frame this recovery task as asking them to give Al-Anon or

Nar-Anon a fair try and to approach meetings with an open mind. Indicate that you will be very interested in hearing about their reactions to meetings and will help them sort out what is useful from what is not as they continue to work with you.

TREATMENT NOTE

Shyness

For the shy or anxious client, the therapist can consider using active facilitation in getting him or her to first meetings. Active facilitation was described at the end of Topic 2.

Readings

Provide Topic 3: Handout 2, Reading Assignments, to your client. Review the handout, while asking the client to read the following between sessions, to extend the benefits of this discussion:

> *Al-Anon Faces Alcoholism*, pages 231–40: "The Nature of the Fellowship" and "The Twelve Steps and Twelve Traditions"[9]
>
> Al-Anon pamphlet *Understanding Ourselves and Alcoholism*[10]

Journal and Handouts

If the client has been maintaining a journal, remind him or her to write down any thoughts or reactions she or he may have to readings, meetings, or to these facilitation sessions, for future discussion. Before the session concludes, provide the client with Topic 3: Handout 3, Journaling Possibility: Describing Your Higher Power. Explain that if he or she decides to keep a journal, he or she may want to consider exploring more deeply the subject of a Higher Power by answering the questions posed in the handout.

Caring Detachment

Suggest one or two specific things the client can do to begin to decrease his or her enabling relationship with the substance abuser and to relate to him or her increasingly via caring detachment. As always, this recovery task should be approached as a collaborative task. Its success depends in large part on the therapist developing a good conceptual understanding of caring detachment, an understanding of the dynamics of the substance abuser–codependent relationship, and an appreciation of the need for most significant others to detach gradually (i.e., to change their relationships to the substance abusers incrementally as opposed to abruptly).

Chapter 10 || Exploring Defenses

Topic 4: Denial

In this session, the therapist presents and discusses the dynamic process of denial as it pertains to both substance abusers and codependents. *Denial is a common psychological defense against loss of control.* Denial can be reflected in inconsistencies between one's words and one's actions and in discrepancies between how individuals view themselves and how they are viewed by others. Although it is a common and understandable reaction to loss of control, denial must be worked through for the substance abuser as well as the significant other to begin their respective recovery processes. This is accomplished in part through educating the significant other about denial, in part through consistently pointing out discrepancies between his or her words and his or her actions or self-views in comparison to others' perceptions of them.

Review (10–15 Minutes)

Once more, begin the session by checking in (i.e., discussing the client's experiences since the last session). Ask whether the client has made any journal entries that he or she would like to share. Then be sure to touch base in each of the following areas:

Journal and Handouts

Did the client maintain a journal or respond to anything contained in the handouts? If so, are there any entries that she or he would like you to read (or would like to read to you)? Take a few minutes to discuss any such journal entries or responses, and encourage the client to continue writing.

Readings

Did the client follow up on the suggested readings? Did she or he read the Al-Anon pamphlet *Understanding Ourselves and Alcoholism?*[1] Did she or he have any reactions to it?

Meetings

How many Al-Anon or Nar-Anon meetings did the client attend? Was she or he comfortable there? If not, why?

What thoughts or emotional reactions did the client have to meetings? Are there any questions about meetings that the therapist can help to answer?

Does the client have any reservations about continuing to attend Al-Anon or Nar-Anon meetings? Ask him or her, "What can you potentially gain from continued participation in Al-Anon or Nar-Anon?"

Caring Detachment

What, if any, actions did the client take since the last session to start or continue the process of caring detachment? What was his or her level of comfort in doing this? What, if any, reaction was there from the substance abuser? Is there anything the therapist can help to clarify with respect to detaching?

New Material (30 Minutes)

Begin by reading one or more of the following passages:

> . . . our drinking careers have been characterized by countless vain attempts to prove we could drink like other people. The idea that somehow, someday he will control and enjoy his drinking is the great obsession of every abnormal drinker.[2]
>
> We have seen the truth demonstrated again and again: "Once an alcoholic, always an alcoholic." Commencing to drink after a period of sobriety, we are in a short time as bad as ever.[3]
>
> Many of us tried to stop using on sheer willpower. This action was a temporary solution. We saw that willpower alone would not work for any length of time.[4]

The above quotes from *Alcoholics Anonymous* and *Narcotics Anonymous* respectively capture the essence of the concept of denial. The alcoholic or addict who is in denial lives with the illusion that she or he can somehow control or limit substance use or use some psychoactive substances "safely." The substance abuser stubbornly refuses to accept the reality of psychological or physical dependence or both.

The lives of alcoholics and drug addicts are typically marked by brief periods of abstinence and countless attempts to limit use. Despite failure after failure on the part of alcoholics or addicts to drink or use like "normal" (i.e., nonaddicted) people, they continue to try to convince themselves (and usually others as well) that they (and not alcohol or other drugs) are in control. Following a period of abstinence, substance abusers begin substance use again, often with every good intention of limiting use, only to find that in short order they are "as bad as ever," as Bill Wilson put it. Subjectively, denial could be described as the refusal to accept this limitation of personal willpower; objectively, it is the inability to effectively control substance use.

Just as substance abusers can engage in denial, so can their significant others. Denial has its parallels in both substance abusers and in their significant others. One spouse of a substance abuser described the situation within a family dealing with addiction this way: "The family denies a [substance use] problem exists at all and excuses it as 'going through a stage,' or blames 'a terrible boss,' or 'too many pressures' to account for the excess [substance use]."[5]

Aside from seeking an excuse to justify substance abuse, as in the preceding quote, a significant other may acknowledge that a substance use problem exists but resist the idea that he or she is essentially powerless to make the drinker or user stop. Both of these forms of denial are common among significant others of substance abusers and are the focus of discussion here.

Denial in the Substance Abuser

The therapist can use the following material as the basis for a discussion of denial as it applies to alcoholics and drug addicts. This will be followed by a discussion of how the concept of denial applies to significant others.

Denial is the term used to refer to the emotional and intellectual difficulties—in a phrase, the internal resistance—people typically experience when confronted with personal limitations or losses. As stated earlier, this resistance tends to be greater in a society such as ours, which has a strong tradition of believing in virtually limitless self-determination. Men and women in our culture react more negatively to the notion of personal limitation and powerlessness than those in cultures that are more accepting of personal limitation.

With respect to alcoholism and addiction, the roots of denial lie in how it feels to be faced with loss of control—in this case, over substance use—as well as the necessity to give it up for good. This is what Step One of the Twelve Steps (acceptance) is about.

Confronting the personal limitations posed by dependency on alcohol or other drugs can cause discomfort in anyone, to be sure. In our society, the idea of powerlessness tends to arouse intense feelings of anxiety, anger, shame, inadequacy, and guilt. Powerlessness can pose a decided threat to self-esteem, as the following exchange between a counselor and a young alcoholic in early treatment reveals.

Anthony was asked by his counselor to tell her how he felt about being powerless over alcohol (if he, indeed, had thought about such powerlessness):

"Not very good," Anthony replied. "It makes me feel less confident."

"Tell me more about that," the counselor said.

"It makes me feel like I've failed," said Anthony.

"Failed how?" asked the counselor.

"Like I'm not strong-willed, not strong-minded enough," Anthony replied.

"And you don't like that idea?" asked the counselor.

"It's definitely not the way I want to think of myself," said Anthony. "And it's not the way I want to be looked at by others."

This interaction, as well as the following case, can be used as vehicles for illustrating some of the points to be made later on. The therapist should feel free to use alternative means of illustrating these concepts—for example, through other cases, stories from the AA or NA Big Books, and so forth. However it is done, *it is very important that the concept of denial and its various forms be illustrated using some concrete examples and not merely presented in abstract terms.*

Barb attempted to avoid coming to terms with her loss of control over substance use as fiercely as any alcoholic might. Her first line of defense was to act angry and offended whenever the subject was brought up by anyone else, such as her husband or her teenaged children. After blowing up, she usually changed the subject, either launching into an attack on the other person or else complaining long and loudly about some other problem, such as finances or her aging and needy parents. In response to the ever-growing list of household chores that went undone, she pleaded fatigue—after all, she said, she worked hard at her job as assistant manager of a clothing store and needed evenings and weekends to unwind. Of course, "unwinding" for Barb meant drinking heavily, starting when she got home.

Not surprisingly, Barb's denial extended outwardly to her behavior as well as inwardly to her own thought processes. For example, she went out of her way to associate with women who drank as much or even more than she did, and then she comforted and defended herself by drawing the comparison between her own use and theirs, concluding that she was merely "average" (and therefore "normal") as compared to her friends. At times, when she felt guilty pouring a fifth or sixth drink, she would tell herself that she "deserved" it, for example, because of the stress of having to endure a job that she thought was beneath her talents. When her children's grades in school began to decline, she attributed that to their lack of motivation, rather than the growing distance between her and them. And so on.

In these and other ways, Barb was able to fend off the complaints of others as well as her own nagging conscience. Meanwhile, the quality of her life and her own health steadily declined. It was only when she faced disciplinary action at work, a husband who was talking about separation, children who were constantly battling with her, and early symptoms of diabetes, that Barb reluctantly took her first hard look at her drinking and her ability to control it.

Discussing Powerlessness

Provide your client with Topic 4: Handout 1, Discussing Powerlessness. Review the handout, and ask the client how it might feel to be powerless over alcohol or drugs. Encourage the client to write her or his replies and to discuss the following questions in session. (Clients may also choose to explore these questions further in their journals at a later time.) Help him or her articulate both emotional and intellectual reactions to the notion of powerlessness by using open-ended questions such as the following:

- How do you think Barb or Anthony, in the preceding examples, felt about the idea of being powerless over substance use?
- How do you think your own loved one feels, emotionally speaking, about the idea of being powerless to control his or her drinking or drug use?
- Have you personally ever felt powerless over something in your life? What were you powerless over, and how did that feel?
- What do you think it would be like to feel that you were losing control of (i.e., becoming powerless over) substance use?

The Seven Forms of Denial

Use Topic 4: Handout 2, The Seven Forms of Denial, which are described in the following paragraphs, to assist in the discussion with your client of these common forms denial takes:

1. Simple denial
2. Minimizing and maximizing
3. Avoidance
4. Rationalizing
5. Distracting
6. Pseudochoice
7. Bargaining

Review the handout, and go on to explain and illustrate the following seven forms of denial:

Simple Denial

It is normal for people to protect themselves from the psychological pain that results from limitation or loss. One of the easiest ways to do this is to deny the reality of the limitation or loss. Simple denial amounts to refusing to face facts: refusing to make the connection between one's own behavior and its consequences or refusing to face up to increasing unmanageability, loss of control over substance use, and physical and psychological dependence. Examples of simple denial of a substance use problem include the following:

- refusing to discuss substance use
- refusing to accurately attribute obvious consequences of substance use: attributing a driving accident to slippery roads or bad tires rather than to driving while intoxicated, attributing trouble on the job to a mean supervisor rather than to daily drug or alcohol abuse, and so on
- rejecting clear evidence of one's own failures to stop or limit substance use

Minimizing and Maximizing

In this form of denial, the individual minimizes his or her own substance use and its consequences by drawing false comparisons between his or her use and that of others. Here are some examples:

- understating the negative consequences of substance use to oneself while simultaneously exaggerating the consequences of others' substance use (e.g., "I spend less than $100 a week on cocaine; Jeff spends that much every day.")
- accusing others of exaggerating one's own use and its negative consequences (e.g., "I'm not as bad as you're making me out to be.")
- grossly overstating others' level of substance use to normalize one's own (e.g., "Joe gets high every day at work, but I just use in the evening.")

Avoidance

Sometimes, alcoholics and addicts avoid coming to terms with their substance use problems by minimizing contact with family members or others who might observe and confront them. In doing so, they try to keep the extent of their relationships with alcohol or other drugs secret. Examples include these:

- the alcoholic who may spend much of his free time at a local "club," consistently come home drunk, but have no one there to witness just how much he drank at the club
- the alcoholic who has spent virtually every evening holed up in some basement workshop, puttering around and drinking until everyone else has gone to bed. (The wife of one such man sensed clearly that her husband was really married to the booze, but he insisted that he was just pursuing his hobby.)

Rationalizing

This form of denial involves finding excuses for substance use. Some of the more common justifications include the following:

- work, family, or marital stress
- depression or anxiety
- physical pain, discomfort, or insomnia
- social pressure ("Everyone else was drinking.")

Distracting

Another way to avoid having to come to terms with one's loss of control over substance use is to distract others anytime the issue comes up by simply changing the subject. Alcoholics and addicts can be remarkably clever at this. A wife may begin a conversation with every intention of talking to her husband about some negative consequence that seems clearly associated with his drinking only to find herself lured into a discussion of their marital problems, his frustrations at work, or problems with their children, for example:

- A particularly clever version of this tactic is to redirect the discussion from the substance abuser to the significant other.
- Many a loved one of a substance abuser has found himself or herself on the defensive, talking about some problem of his or her own, every time he or she tries to confront the substance abuser.

Pseudochoice

In this form of denial, the individual acknowledges excessive substance use or negative consequences of substance use or both, but then he or she attempts to attribute both substance use and its consequences to choice rather than to progressive loss of control, for example:

- A gregarious alcoholic, for instance, may attribute his tendency to get falling-down drunk four or five times a week to his "party personality," thereby implying that his behavior is voluntary (and therefore, under control).
- A stressed-out cocaine abuser may acknowledge getting into trouble at work or with the law but then explain away these consequences of substance use as reflections of his "rebellious personality." Again, the implication is that the user chooses to use cocaine and to act rebelliously. This maneuver attempts to avoid the alternative attribution: that loss of control over cocaine use is responsible for the consequences.

Bargaining

One of the most common forms of denial, bargaining, is agreeing to limit or control either the amount or type of alcohol or other drugs used or when they are used, as opposed to abstaining from use. Bargaining can be thought of as placating—either one's own conscience or the expressed concerns of others. Here are examples:

- One substance abuser told his wife that he would only use cocaine on special occasions. Initially, this meant holidays, but soon, the list of special occasions became very long indeed!
- Other typical examples of bargaining include swearing off some kinds of substances (but not others) or some forms of substances (e.g., hard liquor) as opposed to others (wine or beer) or some routes of administration (e.g., snorting versus injecting heroin).

Behavioral Correlates of Denial

Denial, as a means of resisting acceptance of progressive loss of control over drug or alcohol use, can take on various forms, as described earlier. These forms of denial concern mainly what the substance abuser *says* or *thinks*. These could be called *cognitive* forms of denial.

Denial can also be identified through close observation of the substance abuser's behavior, in other words, with the way she or he acts. It is useful to educate significant others about this so as to support their own beliefs about the substance abusers' drinking or drug problems in the face of denial.

Significant others of substance abusers can expect to encounter stiff resistance to the suggestion that someone is, in fact, addicted. Clever and persistent denial on the part of the substance abuser can inject an element of doubt into the minds of many loved ones. To counter this, and to be able to have confidence in their own perceptions (as opposed to what the substance abusers say), significant others can be taught to recognize other behavioral signs of denial. Therapists, of course, can also use this information when dealing with a resistant substance abuser.

Self-Perception versus Perceptions of Others

The first way in which denial becomes evident on a behavioral level is through the discrepancy between the way substance abusers view themselves and how they are viewed by others. Here is an example:

Victor, a successful professional, had been drinking virtually daily for fifteen years. For almost as long, he had also been smoking marijuana once or twice during the week and virtually every day on the weekend. His wife, Mary, sought help because she was feeling depressed and frustrated. No matter how much she complained to him, he staunchly refused to consider even moderating, much less stopping, either his marijuana use or his drinking. With respect to the former, he insisted that the children did not know he smoked pot, because he was discreet about it. Mary wasn't so sure.

Of primary concern to Mary was the fact that their two sons were getting to an age at which she felt they suspected the truth about their father. They had, for instance, already asked her probing questions about his drug history. She was concerned not only for how it might affect their respect for their father if it were confirmed that he was a pothead or an alcoholic, but she was also worried about the message it would communicate to them: that drinking and smoking marijuana was okay.

Victor agreed (with great reluctance) to see a counselor with Mary. In defending his marijuana use, he said, "It relaxes me. I've always been an intense, distractible person by nature. I'm something of a workaholic. Mary's known that since she's known me. And for years, my smoking was okay with her. She even did some herself, way back when. Smoking a joint or two relaxes me. It actually makes me feel more focused."

Asked if she agreed with Victor's self-assessment, Mary shook her head. "No," she said, "that's not the way I experience Victor when he's high. And it's not the way the kids experience him either. They're getting older now, and they're starting to ask me questions, like, 'Why is Dad so out of it?'"

Mary was encouraged by the therapist to go to Al-Anon meetings and also to honor her perception that smoking pot definitely affected Victor's behavior in ways that, as she put it, "make him a nonentity in the family. It's like I don't really have a husband and the boys don't have a father whenever he's high, but especially on the weekends." She was further encouraged to consider starting to do things with their sons without Victor on weekends if he chose to get high.

In this example, Victor's self-perception—that he was more relaxed and focused on marijuana—was inconsistent with the way his wife and children viewed his behavior. Although she had this perception before, without the validation and support of a third party (the therapist), Mary had backed down in the face of Victor's adamant insistence that pot did not affect him. With that support, she was able to take her first steps toward relating to Victor in a different way and thereby begin a process of recovery that eventually led to Victor becoming clean and sober.

Words versus Actions

Another way in which denial is manifested has to do with discrepancies between what the substance abuser says about his or her substance use and what she or he does. Here is another example:

Doug had been through treatment twice before for alcoholism, and after his last relapse, his wife was close to divorcing him. He told his new counselor, "This time, I finally admit it—I am powerless over alcohol. I have to give it up. No more playing around with ideas of social drinking for me. I know now that I can't drink at all."

These remarks were made in the context of a conjoint session with Doug and his wife, June, and judging by what he said, it appeared that Doug was highly motivated to stop drinking. To further support this statement of acceptance of the First Step of AA, Doug said he was attending three to four AA meetings a week, had been reading the Big Book, and had approached someone to be his sponsor.

All of the behaviors that Doug cited—and that June could confirm were true—could be said to be consistent with Doug's words. He said he was powerless over alcohol, and he was acting in ways consistent with such a belief. However, as this session went on, the therapist also learned that Doug was still seeing some of his old drinking buddies on a regular basis; moreover, he had even met with them at bars! When questioned about the apparent inconsistency between admitting powerlessness over alcohol and visiting friends in a bar, Doug defensively replied that he had ordered only club soda. Still, the therapist pointed out, the fact that Doug would place himself in such a situation in the first place was not consistent with his statement that he was powerless over alcohol. She used this analogy:

> Say that a man told you he was a gambling addict and that he had lost his house and run into debt as a result of it. Say he admitted that he was powerless over his urge to gamble and that once he started he could not be sure he would stop. Suppose he then told you that although he didn't want to gamble any more, he still liked to meet his old gambling buddies for dinner at a casino. Now, would you say this man's actions were consistent with a belief that gambling was a dangerous addictive tendency within him, one that had the power to overpower his own determination not to gamble?

Doug had to admit that in this hypothetical example, the man's actions were not completely consistent with his words: "I guess if he was really afraid of losing everything at a craps table, he wouldn't set foot in a casino." The therapist pointed out that Doug had lost a lot as a result of alcoholism and that if he truly accepted his powerlessness over it, the last place he wanted to hang out would be in a bar. His behavior, the therapist said, was more consistent with resistance to accepting the First Step; in other words, more consistent with denial than acceptance. It reflected, in behavioral terms, a belief on Doug's part in the capacity of his individual willpower to overcome the risks inherent in placing himself in situations in which the risk of a slip was high. Doug could see how this was true. "I suppose it's just a hard pill to swallow," he said. "I mean, this idea that my willpower isn't enough. On some level, I've never wanted to accept it."

Spouses and other concerned significant others should be encouraged to observe substance abusers' actions and to compare their actions to their words. When they discover a discrepancy, this can be a sign of denial. It is *not* necessarily the significant other's responsibility to confront the substance abuser about this each and every time or to break down his or her denial. Rather, this awareness of denial is useful in so far as it can validate the client's own thinking in the face of opposition and denial from the addict. It can also encourage significant others to continue the process of caring detachment and not to be drawn into the substance abusers' denial systems.

The objective in this discussion of the various forms of denial is to be sure the client has an understanding of the common theme:

Denial in all of its forms serves to protect the substance abuser from having to acknowledge a progressive loss of control over substance use. To check that the client understands denial clearly, help him or her identify several specific examples of denial that his or her loved one has actually used. Give the client Topic 4: Handout 3, Writing Exercises, which contains the following two exercises. Review the handout. These exercises can help to sensitize the codependent to denial when he or she encounters it again.

1. In each instance, write down what the substance abuser said and what form of denial it represents:

   Example 1
   What was said: ______________________.
   What form of denial? ______________________

   Example 2
   What was said: ______________________.
   What form of denial? ______________________

   Example 3
   What was said: ______________________.
   What form of denial? ______________________

2. Help the client to identify any specific examples of discrepancies between the substance abuser's statements about his or her substance use and his or her actions. This is not usually difficult to do, especially for significant others of those substance abusers who are still active or in the early stages of recovery.

   Example 1
   Words: ______________ versus actions: ______________

   Example 2
   Words: ______________ versus actions: ______________

   Example 3
   Words: ______________ versus actions: ______________

Denial in Codependents

The process of denial, as it operates in alcoholics and drug addicts, has its parallels in their significant others. The therapist should note this and explain there can be many reasons significant others may be as reluctant to face the reality of addiction as are substance abusers themselves.

To move toward caring detachment, codependents need to become cognizant of two tendencies in particular within themselves. The first is the tendency to buy into the substance abusers' own denial. Give your client Topic 4: Handout 4, Questions on Denial. Review the handout and suggest that after the session the client reply to the questions in more detail in his or her journal or, if he or she is not keeping a journal, in the space provided on the handout. Meanwhile, to explore the client's tendency to agree with the substance abuser's own denial, use open-ended questions such as the following:

- How many times have you bought into your loved one's denial, in other words, believed his or her explanation instead of trusting your own perceptions? Can you give me an example of a time when you believed an excuse you were getting?
- What forms of denial are you particularly likely to buy into? For instance, do you tend to accept rationalizations for drinking or using? Are you gullible with respect to a minimizing and maximizing strategy?

When significant others accept substance abusers' denial, they help create a kind of conspiracy. Sometimes, they do so simply because they, too, do not want to face the fact that their relationships with their loved ones have in a sense been displaced by other relationships—a commitment by the substance abuser to alcohol or drugs. By slipping into a conspiracy of denial the significant others, like the substance abusers, can cling to the comforting illusion that the situations are really not that bad. Conversely, as denial breaks down, the substance abuser and the codependent alike can be flooded with anxiety.

In addition to not wanting to admit that neither they nor the substance abusers can control substance abuse at that time, significant others may hesitate to face up to the true severity of loved ones' substance abuse problems, because they feel guilty or shameful. They might feel guilty because they think they are somehow responsible for the problems and feel shame over the stigma associated with alcoholism and drug addiction. For some, their loved ones' addictions stir up added feelings of shame associated with a parent's addiction. These people may not want to admit to themselves that once again someone they love has been lost to them through addiction.

Another motive for denial in significant others has to do with a reluctance to accept their own personal limitations. Simply put, *as a substance abuser progressively loses control over substance use, so does his or her significant others.* Many codependents doggedly refuse to face this limitation of their own willpower—that they can't stop the substance abusers from drinking or using other drugs—just as substance abusers refuse to face their limitations even in the throes of addiction. For these significant others, letting go of the illusion that they can prevent or contain addiction directly parallels the substance abusers' need to let go of the illusion that they can drink or use like other people. It may be hubris, or it may be anxiety, or perhaps some combination of both that drives this illusion, but in any case, the reality of the codependent's loss of control over the substance abuser directly parallels the reality of the substance abuser's loss of control over substance use. Letting go of any illusion to the contrary is equally important to both parties in the relationship if they are to recover.

Explore the client's motivations for denial by asking questions such as the following:

- Have you often wanted to believe that the extent of your loved one's substance abuse was not really so bad?
- Did it ever disturb you to think that you might be losing your loved one to alcohol or other drugs, in other words, that the relationship with alcohol or drugs was becoming more important than his or her relationship with you?

- Have you believed at times that it was within your power to get your loved one to stop or control his or her substance use?
- What factors within you might motivate you to want to avoid facing up to the reality of your loved one's addiction and the fact that you are both out of control of his or her substance use? For example, if this were true, what could it mean for your relationship? How might it affect your standard of living? If you have children, how could it affect them?
- Would you feel embarrassed or ashamed about your loved one's addiction or your powerlessness over it? Is it easier to think of it as something else?
- Would facing the reality of addiction mean facing up to a problem of major proportions in your life, one that might prove overwhelming?
- Would facing this reality of your life as it is now remind you of something unpleasant from your own past?
- Have you ever felt guilty (i.e., responsible for) your loved one's substance use? In what way do you imagine you could be responsible for it?
- How do you feel if you think about the idea that you cannot stop your loved one from drinking or using?

Summing Up

Sum up this session by asking the client to tell you the most important thing he or she learned from this discussion. You might want to point out that in Al-Anon and Nar-Anon the client will find people who have shared his or her experience—who, for instance, have had to come to terms with the limits of their willpower and who have found themselves caught with substance abusers in the webs of denial. These men and women can offer support and guidance both in living with a substance abuser and in beginning the process of recovery.

Recovery Tasks (5 Minutes)

The recovery tasks to be suggested are as follows:

Meetings

Continue to suggest to the client that she or he attend Al-Anon or Nar-Anon meetings with the specific suggestion that he or she attend a minimum of two meetings per week. Active facilitation, as described earlier, can be used at any time to assist this process.

Suggest to the client that he or she listen particularly closely to two types of members at meetings who impress him or her: newcomers (persons like him- or herself) and also old-timers (those who have been active in Al-Anon or Nar-Anon for a relatively long time)—in other words, people he or she respects and would want to emulate. The goal for the therapist is to encourage the client to begin to bond to those in the fellowship through contact with these two groups. Old-timers—seasoned Al-Anon or Nar-Anon members—are good candidates for becoming the newcomer's first sponsor.

Telephone and Internet Therapy

Make a specific suggestion that the client get the names and phone numbers or e-mail addresses of three or four same-sex Al-Anon or Nar-Anon members and that he or she try calling, texting, or e-mailing two such people each week. Suggest that it is best if he or she get the contact information of two relative newcomers and two old-timers who have made a favorable impression. If necessary, explain again to the client that this telephone therapy is a long-standing tradition within Al-Anon and Nar-Anon (as well as AA and NA) and that experienced Al-Anon or Nar-Anon members will welcome his or her interest.

TREATMENT NOTE

The Socially Shy Client

If the client seems excessively shy or uneasy about the idea of getting phone numbers or making calls, explore his or her anxiety by asking whether this has been a problem for him or her in the past.

Most socially anxious people describe themselves as having been shy for most of their lives. It can be reassuring to let the shy client know that many Al-Anon and Nar-Anon members are also shy at first and can relate to this problem and also that an important tradition within Twelve Step fellowships is to reach out and connect to others. The therapist might want to either role-play or talk through one such icebreaker phone call or e-mail. The agenda for these first calls can be simple:

> Hi, my name is ________________. I was at the meeting on ________________. I'm a newcomer, and I thought I would just reach out to make contact. Normally, I'm kind of a shy person, but these days, I know I need to start reaching out.

Readings

Give Topic 4: Handout 5, Reading Assignments, to the client, which you can review with him or her.

The following readings are suggested as a follow-up for this topic:

> *Al-Anon Faces Alcoholism,* pages 170–73: "My Brother Is an Alcoholic"; pages 147–51: "Al-Anon Helped Me to Understand My Wife's Problem"; pages 246–55: "Other Tools of the Program"[6]

Journal and Handouts

Encourage the client to continue to make journal entries about his or her reactions to sessions, to meetings, to handouts, and to readings, and to use these entries as grist for the mill at the next session. Provide the client with Topic 4: Handout 6, Journaling Possibility: Exploring Your Own Denial, in case he or she wants to respond more fully to the questions about letting go of illusions in his or her journal.

Caring Detachment

As before, the therapist works collaboratively with the client to come up with one or two specific things she or he can do toward decreasing her or his enabling relationship with the substance abuser and toward moving the relationship instead in the direction of caring detachment. Always keep in mind that detaching as a way of relating to the substance abuser is something that is best shaped incrementally. No matter how minor, a response to the substance abuser that represents caring detachment instead of enabling is likely to elicit a reaction. Caring detachment reflects honesty on the part of the codependent plus a willingness to allow the substance abuser to have the dignity of his or her disease without taking over responsibility for the addiction or for recovery. *Successful detachment almost always disrupts the status quo in the substance abuser–codependent relationship.*

Chapter 11 || The Relationship Between Denial and Enabling

Topic 5: Enabling

The goal of this session is to explain to the client how denial, as discussed in Topic 4, is connected to enabling as a relational pattern. Both denial and enabling are based in the conscious or unconscious belief that the significant other can somehow control, or at least contain, a substance abuse problem and its consequences. Enabling reflects resistance to Step One of Al-Anon and Nar-Anon, which concerns the concept of *acceptance*—a topic that will be covered in the next session.

Review (10–15 Minutes)

Begin the session as usual by devoting the first ten to fifteen minutes to a discussion of the client's experiences since the last session. Be sure to briefly cover each of the following areas:

Journal and Handouts

Did the client maintain a journal or respond to anything contained in the handouts? If so, are there any entries or responses that she or he would like you to read (or would like to read to you)? Take a few minutes to discuss any such journal entries or responses, and encourage the client to continue writing.

Readings

Did the client follow up on the suggested readings? What reactions or questions does she or he have?

Meetings

How many Al-Anon or Nar-Anon meetings did the client attend? What thoughts and emotional reactions did the client have to the meetings? Are there any questions the therapist can help to answer?

Does the client have any reservations about continuing to attend Al-Anon or Nar-Anon meetings?

Telephone and Internet Therapy

Did the client follow up on the therapist's suggestion to get and use three or four Al-Anon or Nar-Anon members' phone numbers or e-mail addresses? Is there anything that can be done to facilitate this?

Caring Detachment

What action(s) has the client taken since the last session to start or continue the process of moving from enabling toward caring detachment? What was his or her level of comfort in taking these steps? What, if any, reaction was there from the substance abuser?

New Material (30 Minutes)

The therapist should be thoroughly familiar with the material that follows and should use it as a guide in engaging the client in a discussion of the concept of enabling.

Enabling: An Overview

Enabling can be defined as any and all behaviors by significant others that have unintentionally facilitated substance abusers' continued substance use. Enabling, as a relational dynamic between the codependent and the substance abuser, unintentionally promotes the progression of the substance abuser's relationship with alcohol or other drugs. At best, enabling maintains the status quo within the substance abuser–codependent relationship, although, over time, it inevitably leads to a diluting of the quality of that relationship.

Often a hallmark of enabling is that, in one way or another, it helps the drinker or drug user avoid or minimize negative consequences related to substance use, be they physical, legal, occupational, or relational consequences. In other words, as the word *enable* implies, enablers provide the means, the excuses, and the safety nets that allow alcoholics or addicts to continue substance use. This is poignantly described in the following description of a mother's response to her teenage daughter's substance use:

> The convulsions she had at home were so thoroughly covered up by me that she could not remember them the next day. I massaged her, poured honey down her throat, soothed her, and applied cold compresses. It proved futile to tell her what had occurred, because within a short time, the drinking began

> again. It is now clear to me that it is necessary for the alcoholic to feel the pain. But it was I who bore my daughter's pain. I deprived her of some of the incentive to take constructive action for the consequences of her drinking. In essence, I took on the responsibility and the consequences of her disease.[1]

Yet another way to look at enabling is that it represents indulgence or pampering of the addict. It can be motivated out of caring and concern, as in the previous example; alternatively, it may reflect the enabler's own personality and his or her desire to deny the reality of addiction, as the following account by the wife of an alcoholic suggests:

> False pride helped me create a prison in which I lived for the next 20 years. I wanted to be proud of our marriage and our family (we had six sons), so I buried the resentment and began pretending. By the time our sons were in their twenties, one had gone through treatment for chemical dependency. I also realized that three of our other sons were chemical abusers. I didn't want to believe this was happening or that alcohol was the problem. So I kept on pretending, and I played the role of caretaker for the whole family. I assumed it was my job to control them, make them happy, keep them from hurting and out of trouble. The family seemed to agree. Their dependent personalities accepted such mothering and only occasionally did they rebel.[2]

As another example of enabling, consider Elaine, age fifty-five, who held a responsible position and supported two adult sons, both of whom were alcoholics. She had divorced their alcoholic father when the boys were young, not so much because he drank, but because he was chronically unfaithful. She sought help for a common and understandable reason: chronic frustration in coping with her sons. She was feeling "soul tired," as she put it: discouraged and disheartened. One of her sons was now living with her and was unemployed and unmotivated. The other son lived on his own, but he was also very dependent on her for anything from money for booze to a decent meal.

Elaine asked her therapist outright for a solution to her dilemma and distress. She had no qualms about sharing her feelings of hopelessness and admitting her sense of defeat. She hoped the therapist would miraculously cure the problem. She said she had been thinking about relocating to another state just to escape the situation. The therapist pointed out that because her sons were clearly dependent on her, they would, no doubt, follow Elaine if she did move. She laughed at that, but took the point well. The bottom line—the reality of her utter frustration—was clearly well understood by her and her therapist.

Elaine was a strong enabler. Her actions were motivated out of love, yet virtually everything she did supported the status quo and undermined any motivation for either of her sons to change, while allowing their relationships with alcohol and drugs to progress from that of friendship to commitment. She worried that her younger son—the one who lived at home—might be on the verge of becoming a slave to cocaine.

Elaine fed and housed her sons, did their laundry, lent them money. It was during her fourth therapy session—when Elaine talked about being a single parent—that Elaine's intense guilt became apparent to her therapist, along with the role that guilt played in her enabling:

> After my divorce, I never did find a man I could believe in enough to want to marry again. It's a common story, I know, but I just seemed to attract more of the same! Anyway, it bothered me at times that the boys never had a proper father. I tried my best never to deny them. I'm the kind of person who hates to say no. I remember one time, though, when my youngest was ten and he wanted to go to this weekend thing with these older boys, and I said no. I felt he was just too young. He got really upset. It hurt me to say no, but I had to do it. Sometimes, I wonder if that didn't affect him in some way.

How ironic that this mother actually blamed herself for her son's addiction because of the one time when she denied him! Of course, pursuing the goal of caring detachment would require Elaine to move in just the opposite direction: to learn to deny more often. Only by doing so, could she begin to break the cycle of indulgence and restructure her relationships with her grown sons so as to be that of one adult to another adult, instead of the parent-child relationships they had grown so used to. To accomplish this, it was evident that Elaine would need a great deal of support, not only from the therapist but from the fellowship of Al-Anon.

However *enabling* is defined, the bottom line is that it serves to mitigate the consequences of alcoholism or drug addiction. In this way it has the (perhaps unintended) effect of allowing the disease of addiction to progress. *Without their systems of enablers, most substance abusers would bottom out more quickly.*

The therapist should ask the client whether she or he has heard the term *enabling*, and if so, what it means to him or her. Check that the client has a clear understanding of this concept in light of the material presented earlier. Reading the preceding passages and paraphrasing the definition of *enabling* given earlier can help the client better grasp this concept. Then illustrate enabling by using a few examples such as the following. *Enabling* is

- making excuses (covering up) for the substance abuser when she or he is drunk or high and would otherwise get into trouble
- giving an alcoholic "only a little" alcohol in the hope that she or he won't want any more (or giving a drug abuser "only a little" money when she or he asks for it)
- giving in to demands to "borrow" money or paying bills that the substance abuser has run up because of impaired judgment or impulsivity when using
- calling in "sick" for the person who, in truth, is hung over or crashing after alcohol or drug use
- conspiring with the substance abuser to accept his or her denial in whatever form it takes
- excusing or justifying hostility, abuse, or other inappropriate behavior that results from substance abuse

- accepting guilt-ridden apologies time and again for harm or damage done while under the influence of alcohol or drugs and believing it will never happen again
- making runs to liquor stores (or drug dealers) to keep an alcoholic or addict off the street (possibly to avoid arrest or an accident)
- defending an alcoholic or addict to others or apologizing for the alcoholic or addict for inappropriate or irresponsible behavior
- giving a substance abuser liquor or drugs to quiet him or her or keep the peace

The common theme in all of these examples is that enabling in any of its forms has the effect of helping the alcoholic or drug addict avoid the real issue—which is his or her substance abuse—in large part, by helping minimize the consequences of such abuse. In time, the substance abuser–codependent relationship settles into a stable but highly dysfunctional pattern and becomes progressively more of a parent-child relationship than an adult-to-adult relationship. Meanwhile, two things happen:

- the substance abuser's relationship with alcohol or drugs deepens
- the codependent's physical and psychological health steadily deteriorate

An irony of enabling is that the consequences that are minimized are the very ones that might help motivate the substance abuser to think about changing; therefore, enabling undermines any such motivation. All the while, the codependent becomes progressively more responsible for the substance abuser, instead of the substance abuser taking responsibility for himself or herself.

The Enabling Inventory

To be certain that the client clearly understands the concept of enabling and can relate to it in the context of his or her relationship with the substance abuser, elicit several examples of enabling and use them to construct an Enabling Inventory. A blackboard or flip chart is helpful for doing this. (If neither are available, a large sheet of paper will suffice). In addition, provide Topic 5: Handout 1, The Enabling Inventory, to the client so he or she can make notes and keep a copy of the inventory after it is finished. To complete the Enabling Inventory, have the client list three specific examples in which he or she has unintentionally allowed the substance abuser or himself or herself to do the following three things:

1. Gain access to alcohol or drugs

   Example 1: ________________________________

   Example 2: ________________________________

   Example 3: ________________________________

2. Minimize or avoid physical, occupational, or relational consequences of substance use

   Example 1: ________________________________

   Example 2: ________________________________

   Example 3: ________________________________

3. Progress in his or her relationship with alcohol or drugs (from "casual friend" to "relationship" to "commitment" to "slave")

   Example 1: ________________________________

   Example 2: ________________________________

   Example 3: ________________________________

Enabling and Denial

Significant others enabling substance abusers can be thought of as a complementary process to denial in substance abusers, in that the one supports the other. The underlying dynamic in denial and enabling is that in each behavior, individuals resist facing the reality of progressive loss of control over substance use. The potential alcoholic, for example, continues to hold onto the illusion that he or she can drink like "normal" people, despite increasing evidence to the contrary. Meanwhile, the codependent either continues to believe this same myth—that the substance abuser can drink or use like the nonalcoholic or nonaddict—or else to believe that he or she can get the substance abuser to stop drinking or can contain the damage caused by addiction.

This latter thought—be it conscious or merely implied in the significant other's actions—rests on the assumption that a concerned significant other can indeed somehow control a substance abuser's substance abuse. In reality, as addiction progresses, significant others who are caught up in an enabling dynamic take more and more responsibility for the substance abusers in their lives, who, in turn, become increasingly irresponsible and immature. As the substance abuser's relationship to alcohol or drugs becomes more intimate and committed, his or her relationship with the codependent changes, with the codependent increasingly taking on the role of parent.

It is important, from the point of view of motivating significant others to give Al-Anon or Nar-Anon or both a try that they understand, on both an intellectual and a gut level, this central concept of enabling, how it parallels denial, and how it undermines any possibility for recovery. *If the client appears to be having difficulty grasping this concept, the facilitator may need to return to it repeatedly in future sessions, each time illustrating it concretely through the client's self-reported actions and contrasting it with what caring detachment would look like.*

The Dynamics of Enabling

Enabling is fairly obvious as it is revealed in behavior. In contrast, the underlying motivations for enabling may be complex and less apparent. Although enabling typically has the effect of allowing the substance abuser to drink or use, most people enable, not because they actually want the substance abusers to continue substance use but out of desire to protect or shelter the substance abusers, desire to preserve relationships, feelings of guilt, or sense of duty. The motives for enabling are benign and loving, even though they have the effect in the long run of being destructive to the substance abuser, the codependent, and their relationship.

It can be useful in promoting caring detachment to get the client to think about and identify some of his or her underlying motivations for enabling. One or more of the following statements apply to most clients' experiences. Provide Topic 5: Handout 2 , Checklist 1: Enabling, to your client and have him or her check which of the following behaviors most closely relate to the client's own enabling actions (suggest also that the client take this home and review it from time to time):

- On some level, I keep thinking that it will make a difference if I keep on doing what I've been doing.
- I feel that this is the only way to save our relationship.
- I think I will eventually convince him (her) to stop.
- I'm afraid of what will happen to him (her) if I stop doing what I'm doing.
- I feel partly responsible for the problem.

How do enablers feel? Often they feel guilty because they secretly worry they have somehow caused or contributed to the problems surrounding another's substance abuse. This is a hidden fear that many alcoholics and addicts play on to promote enabling. Many partners and family members of alcoholics and addicts report deep feelings of self-doubt about their adequacy in their relationship with the substance abuser.

Enablers are often fearful and anxious because they don't know what could happen if they let go of trying to control a substance abuser. What would be the impact, for example, on a marriage, or on a family's financial security, if they stopped enabling?

Enablers also experience considerable frustration and feel angry because the substance abuser won't change, won't listen to advice, and continues to drink or use other drugs. Like the substance abusers, enablers find themselves repeating scenes they hoped would never happen again: calling in sick for the hungover spouse, making excuses to family or friends for inappropriate behavior, cleaning up messes, and so on.

Sooner or later, enablers experience hopelessness and feel depressed as a result of continued substance use and the progressive unmanageability of not only the substance abusers' lives but also their own lives and relationships. As an inner sense of hopelessness sets in, many significant others eventually write off both the substance abusers and the relationships, emotionally speaking, even if they don't actually leave the relationships. They give up seeking intimacy, love, and even reliability from the substance abuser, accepting instead his or her primary commitment to alcohol or other drugs.

In the end, feelings of alienation take root as estrangement hardens. Eventually, this state of affairs will undermine the spiritual, psychological, and physical health of the significant other. Not a few enablers have turned to alcohol or other drugs themselves as a compensation for the quiet desperation and loneliness that plagues them.

Try to get the client to identify the various emotions he or she feels with respect to the substance abuse problem. Provide Topic 5: Handout 3, Checklist 2: Enabling, to the client and ask the client to check which of the following emotions seem familiar (suggest the client take this home and use it as a measurement tool to assess his or her feelings from time to time):

- *guilty*, because of the fear that the client is somehow responsible for a loved one's problems
- *anxious*, because the client's life is becoming progressively more unmanageable as a result of his or her loved one's substance abuse
- *angry*, because the client's efforts at stopping or containing the problem have been frustrated
- *depressed*, because things seem out of control
- *hopeless* and ready to give up on love, intimacy, and commitment
- *alienated*, because the client's profound sense of defeat has hardened into resignation at having lost a relationship to alcohol or drugs

These are all feelings and states of being clients will eventually discover that others at Al-Anon and Nar-Anon meetings have also experienced. However, newcomers are especially prone to sinking into hopeless despair, which makes them vulnerable to dropping out of Al-Anon or Nar-Anon prematurely if they keep such feelings to themselves (as opposed to sharing them at meetings and opening themselves up to support). Being able to acknowledge and express such feelings to the therapist, therefore—particularly early on in his or her involvement in a Twelve Step fellowship—can be critical to a client's ability to bond to the fellowship in the long run.

Summing Up

Ask the client to summarize what she or he got out of this session. Particular attention should be paid (1) to see that clients understand enabling and can identify at least a few specific ways they have enabled their substance abusers, (2) to assess clients' abilities to identify their possible motives for enabling, and (3) to help clients express their feelings about their own relationships with the substance abusers and about the substance abusers' relationships with drugs or alcohol.

Recovery Tasks (5 Minutes)

The suggested recovery tasks for this topic are as follows:

Meetings

Continue to suggest that the client attend Al-Anon and Nar-Anon meetings with the specific suggestion that he or she attend two meetings per week. Active facilitation, as described earlier, can be used at any time to assist this process.

Again, suggest to the client that he or she listen particularly closely to two types of members at meetings: newcomers like themselves and old-timers who have been active in Al-Anon or Nar-Anon for a relatively long time and who impress him or her as people he or she would like to know better. The goal for the therapist is to consistently encourage and coach the client to establish connections to other newcomers and to seasoned Al-Anon or

Nar-Anon members so as to facilitate the process of bonding to the fellowship.

Telephone and Internet Therapy

Continue to encourage the client to accept and give contact information and to establish a network of Al-Anon or Nar-Anon contacts. Use role-playing if necessary to facilitate this.

Readings

Give the client Topic 5: Handout 4, Reading Assignments, and review the assignments with him or her.

The following readings are recommended, along with any others that the client may have discovered—for example, by going to meetings:

> *Al-Anon Faces Alcoholism*, pages 31–36: "Detachment and Growth"; pages 134–39: "I Learned to Love"[3]

Journal and Handouts

Encourage the client to continue to make journal entries about his or her reactions to sessions, to meetings, to handouts, and to readings, and to use these entries as grist for the mill at the next session.

Caring Detachment

Suggest one or two specific things the client can do to decrease his or her enabling behavior and instead practice caring detachment. Continue to reinforce these efforts to change as ones that will, in time, change the nature of the substance abuser–codependent relationship, moving it from an unhealthy dependency (parent-child) toward mutual respect (adult-adult). Help the client identify and work through any feelings of guilt or anxiety that might undermine his or her efforts to detach.

Chapter 12 || Understanding Step One

Topic 6: Acceptance

The goal of this session is to explore the First Step of Al-Anon and Nar-Anon, which has to do with what is commonly referred to as *acceptance* in the recovery community. In the discussion of new material, the therapist will ask the client how she or he has tried to control or contain the addiction process, how that has worked, and whether the client is now ready to try another way. Reactions to powerlessness and unmanageability will be explored in depth here to enhance the client's motivation to use Al-Anon or Nar-Anon.

Review (10–15 Minutes)

Begin the session, as in previous ones, by devoting about ten to fifteen minutes checking in with the client. Be sure to touch on each of the following areas:

Journal and Handouts

Did the client maintain a journal or respond to anything contained in the handouts? If so, are there any entries or responses that she or he would like you to read (or would like to read to you)? Take a few minutes to discuss any such journal entries or responses, and encourage the client to continue writing.

Readings

Did the client follow up on any suggested readings? What reactions or questions does she or he have? Has the client discovered any new readings that she or he would like to share?

Meetings

How many Al-Anon or Nar-Anon meetings did the client attend since the last session?

What thoughts and emotional reactions has the client had to meetings? Has he or she found people with whom to identify?

Are there issues that could be addressed that would facilitate the client's active participation in and bonding with Al-Anon or Nar-Anon?

Does the client have any reservations about continuing to attend Al-Anon or Nar-Anon meetings? Can any of these be worked through?

TREATMENT NOTE

Focusing on Similarities

Often individuals who consistently report feeling unconnected or uncomfortable at meetings are doing one of two things that undermine the bonding process. First, they may be attending a meeting that does not happen to be conducive to identification. The parents of a young adult drug addict, for example, found themselves unable to relate to the one Nar-Anon meeting that was available in their area. Virtually all of the other members of this group were either wives or girlfriends of heroin addicts and most were considerably younger than they were. On learning this, their counselor suggested they try a couple of Al-Anon meetings, including one that the counselor knew was specifically for parents. It was a little more inconvenient, but the results were very positive. This couple reported they felt they finally found a "home base."

Indeed, every concerned significant other, like every addict, needs to be able to find a home group to use as a foundation for his or her recovery. Twelve Step fellowships are highly diverse. There are so many different groups and different formats that—with a little persistence—it is all but impossible *not* to be able to find at least one meeting in which a newcomer could identify with at least some members.

Difficulties with bonding can also stem from a significant other's tendency to focus attention on group members with whom he or she cannot relate while largely ignoring those with whom they could identify. This may reflect a conscious or unconscious resistance to bonding, in which case, the significant other can be expected to persist in focusing on members he or she sees as very different from himself or herself, despite the counselor's best efforts to work through this. Alternately, this problem has also been found to be correctable in many cases through effective coaching by a skilled counselor. One common problem for some newcomers is a seeming compulsion to focus all of their attention on another group member who irritates or annoys the client in some way. On further inquiry, the counselor may discover that the client does this in other group situations as well.

One newcomer to Al-Anon, for example, expressed frustration with a male member of the group she attended whom she thought was very sexist. Each time she went, she found herself sitting in the meeting stewing over everything this man said. Meanwhile, when asked by her counselor, she could never recall much of what anyone else had said. The counselor suggested that the newcomer either try some different meetings or else focus on what others were saying and then asked the client to report back in their next session. The newcomer took the second option, with good results. At the next session with the therapist, she was even able to laugh at herself: "You know, I realized that there were a lot of other good people at that meeting, but I wasn't open to them. Instead, I kept fixating on this guy. Then I realized that I was having trouble letting go of him, just like I have trouble letting go of my husband!"

Another newcomer kept complaining to his therapist that the meetings he went to included many women and none of the men in attendance was a professional like himself. He was advised to try looking beyond these differences and focusing instead on identifying with the core story of codependence, which has to do with progressive loss of control, unmanageability, and eventual alienation from the addict. Conversely, recovery in codependents is a story of slow but steady movement toward caring detachment. In this case, that meant, among other things, allowing his wife to have the dignity of her disease: to experience its natural consequences, which included his changed feelings for her (which for years he largely avoided thinking about and had never shared with her) and to work on moving from the dependency of an enabling relationship toward the mutual respect that comes from caring detachment. As he began to focus on the members' shared core story, instead of what sex they were or what they did for a living, this newcomer found that he could very easily identify and bond with this group and use it as a base of support for detaching.

Telephone and Internet Therapy

Has the client accepted and used any contact information? If not, what is the source of the resistance? Can anything be done to facilitate this?

New Material (30 Minutes)

Begin the discussion by reading the First Step of Al-Anon aloud:

> We admitted we were powerless over alcohol—that our lives had become unmanageable.[1]

Point out that this Step, which is identical to the First Step of AA (as well as that of NA, which simply substitutes the word *drugs* for *alcohol*), includes two related concepts that are central to why Twelve Step fellowships like Al-Anon, Nar-Anon, AA, and NA exist. These concepts are powerlessness and unmanageability, which are related because it is increasing powerlessness over substance use that makes life progressively more unmanageable for substance abusers and their significant others alike.

Discuss these ideas with the client, beginning with a discussion of powerlessness.

Powerlessness

The concept of powerlessness is a charged one—psychologically and emotionally. Powerlessness is threatening. As pointed out earlier, powerlessness is an idea that runs counter to our cultural ethic, which embraces radical individualism and stresses individual achievement over interdependence and collective effort. In this cultural context, admitting powerlessness over anything, including substance use, can be seen as a crushing personal defeat (and something to be ashamed of). It is, in fact, regarded that way by many substance abusers and codependents. On the other hand, accepting and admitting powerlessness can be seen simply as a statement of humility: that personal willpower alone has not been successful in one's efforts to effectively limit or control substance use and that negative consequences of substance use continue to accrue. Interestingly enough, many people report that while they mightily resisted the idea of being powerless over addiction for a long time, once they took that important First Step, they experienced not anxiety or hopelessness, but relief (at being able to let go of the burden of trying to change the addict) and a certain amount of hope (that the fellowship could help them).

Engage the client in a discussion of powerlessness and these two very different ways of approaching it. The goal of this dialogue is to help the client identify which reaction—horror and shame or humble acceptance—he or she has to the idea of admitting powerlessness. A useful context for this discussion is the many ways in which the client has tried to control or contain his or her loved one's substance use. Topic 6: Handout 1, Admitting Powerlessness, contains a list of open-ended questions that can be useful for this purpose. Have the client take the handout home and add any additional ideas or responses that weren't discussed during the session:

- Can you remember how you reacted when the thought first occurred to you that ___(insert name)___ had or was developing a substance use problem? What did you think? What was your emotional reaction?
- How have you tried to control or limit ______________'s substance use? Describe several specific things you've done. *Note: The therapist might want to prompt the client here by mentioning common things that significant others typically do, such as threatening, removing alcohol or drugs from the house, arguing, pleading, warning, etc.*
- What was the outcome of each of the efforts you made to get ______________ to stop substance use?
- How does it make you feel when your efforts don't work?
- When did you start to feel powerless over ___________'s substance use?

Some people have a much harder time than others admitting they are powerless over things, including being powerless to control someone else's substance abuse. How difficult is this for the client to admit?

TREATMENT NOTE

Powerlessness Versus Helplessness

In this discussion of powerlessness, it can be very important to include some discussion of the difference between powerlessness and helplessness. This point has been made before, but it is worth repeating again now: the client needs to appreciate the fact that although she or he may be powerless to force the drinker or drug user to stop, she or he is not helpless when it comes to stopping the enabling and to changing the dynamics within the relationship that only serve to prolong the problem. Significant others are also not helpless with respect to learning to take care of their own health and well-being, which usually suffers as a consequence of addiction. That is an integral part of caring detachment as opposed to enabling. Active involvement in Al-Anon or Nar-Anon or both is the preferred source of support to work toward both of these goals.

Unmanageability

Life for both substance abusers and their loved ones becomes progressively unmanageable as addiction progresses through its several stages from social use to compulsive use of alcohol or other drugs. Unmanageability is the direct result of growing powerlessness over substance use. The therapist can use the following case (or another one drawn from his or her experience that serves to illustrate the same points) to facilitate a discussion of unmanageability:

Bob and Kathy, a couple married for twenty years, went to a counselor, ostensibly for help with marital difficulties. Although the issue was initially obscured by discussions and arguments about money, children, and sex, it became apparent after a while that Bob had a significant drinking problem that needed to be evaluated. He was asked to come in individually for a session to talk about this. Reluctantly, he agreed.

It turned out that Bob had several signs of alcohol dependency. He had a powerful tolerance, drank daily, and had experienced a number of drinking-related consequences, not the least of which was a seriously strained marriage. He had hypertension serious enough to require medication. The counselor also discovered that he was in trouble at work as a consequence of drinking—a consequence he had kept secret from his wife. All things considered, Bob had a commitment to alcohol that was clearly taking priority more and more over his commitments at home and at work.

Bob was reluctant to change the focus of therapy from his troubled marriage to his drinking. This was interpreted as part of his denial. He was assured that his concerns about the marriage were legitimate and would be dealt with, but first, the counselor said, he needed to do something about his drinking or risk losing his job, possibly his marriage, and definitely his health.

The story of Bob's private struggle for control over alcohol was a testament to stubborn determination as much as it was a classic story of the power of addiction. Having started out sipping beers stolen from the refrigerator as a youth barely ten years old, Bob had been drinking continuously for thirty years. But things didn't get bad, he said, until after he was married and the kids were born. Two things happened then. First, he felt obligated to stay in a job that paid well but that he had previously intended to leave. Second, his relationship with Kathy, in his words, became diluted (as marriages often do at that point) as a consequence of the demands of family life.

It was around this time, after his younger child, a daughter, was born, that Bob developed the habit of having a cocktail or two every night after work before dinner. For a long time, Kathy went along with this, although she did notice that a cocktail or two eventually became three, four, or more. Her own father had been a drinker and so, for a long time, Bob's behavior did not strike Kathy as particularly abnormal. Ironically, she took his ability to drink others under the table—in other words, his tolerance—to be a good thing. In her naïveté, she believed that his ability to hold his liquor was actually a sign that Bob could *not* become addicted.

As time went on, the process of addiction gradually set in. Instead of eating in the company cafeteria, Bob found himself going out for lunch two or three times a week. Of course, he had a couple of beers every time. By the time he got home, he was anxious to "relax"—his euphemism for having cocktails. Kathy and the kids soon found that anything that stood between Bob and his cocktails made him irritable. He didn't want to be bothered with problems until he was "relaxed." Of course, by the time he was relaxed, Bob was also intoxicated. That made him emotionally unstable and prone to losing his temper. So the rest of the family eventually learned to avoid him. Kathy took to solving most of the household problems by herself or else she let them go. The kids, meanwhile, led their own lives and had minimal communication with their father.

Although he was hesitant to admit it for a long time, Bob had struggled long and hard (and ultimately unsuccessfully) to privately control his drinking. He hadn't wanted to be like his own father: a quiet drunk who was less flamboyant than Bob in his drinking but who had liked his liquor, nonetheless, and who had also been a social isolate and a "nonfactor," which is how Bob described his role as a parent.

Even though Bob had never read the Big Book, the methods he eventually disclosed that he had tried in his long struggle to control his drinking sounded like something right out of it: drinking only wine, drinking only beer (no cocktails) at lunch, drinking from a smaller glass, adding more ice cubes to his cocktails, and so on. All the while, he was conscious on some level of gradually losing control, yet he continued to convince himself that he was really all right.

By the time he and Kathy came for marital therapy, Bob had managed to fall two years behind on their tax returns and they owed the government several thousand dollars. According to Kathy, the house they lived in was becoming increasingly dilapidated on account of maintenance projects he kept putting off doing himself or hiring someone else to accomplish. Their son, who had just turned eighteen, was failing half of his courses in college; meanwhile, according to Bob, his daughter hated him and alternately fought with and ridiculed him. He had not received a merit raise for three years at work, and his job evaluations, once outstanding, were now routinely average. His boss was openly critical of his work, and Bob was convinced that the man was out to get him. Worst of all, he had suffered the humiliation of being called on the carpet as a result of having alcohol on his breath and had been warned that a second such incident would lead to disciplinary action. On top of all this, Kathy was sexually turned off, which left Bob feeling not only frustrated but filled with self-pity that only made him want to drink all the more.

Like Bob, every alcoholic's and addict's life is a story of steadily increasing unmanageability leading in the end to powerlessness. As the First Step of Al-Anon and Nar-Anon (as well as this story) makes clear, unmanageability affects not only the alcoholic or addict but all those who are close to him or her.

Engage the client in a discussion of how his or her loved one's alcohol or drug abuse has made both their lives increasingly unmanageable. If necessary, prompt the client's memory with information you've gathered during earlier sessions. By this point in the FRP, the therapist should have a fairly thorough knowledge of the client's relationship with the substance abuser and should have ample concrete examples of progressive unmanageability. The therapist may want to actually list several ways in which she or he believes the client's life has become increasingly unmanageable.

TREATMENT NOTE

Acceptance and Depression

Before going on to discuss recovery tasks, the therapist might want to take some time to check in with the client regarding his or her emotional state at this point. Acceptance of one's powerlessness over addiction carries with it the potential to elicit feelings of depression and, in extreme cases, despair. This makes sense if one considers that, although denial tends to promote enabling, it also protects the codependent from the harsh reality of addiction and powerlessness. When the wall of denial falls, significant others may experience relief but also intense anxiety. Check this out with the client. Although it is important to validate (and not avoid) some anxiety and sadness in the client—which is a realistic reaction to Step One—it is also important not to allow the client to sink into hopelessness.

If there is a sense that the client may be feeling helpless and hopeless, take special care to emphasize that Al-Anon and Nar-Anon were founded to help significant others of substance abusers help one another deal with precisely what the client is going through now. If necessary, point out again that *powerlessness* is not synonymous with *helplessness* and that facing up to unmanageability and turning to Al-Anon or Nar-Anon can actually be a relief.

If the client has been attending Al-Anon or Nar-Anon, the therapist would, of course, encourage him or her to continue participating in these fellowships. On the other hand, if the client has been resistant to Al-Anon or Nar-Anon, this is a perfect time to again urge him or her to give it a try, in the interest of reaching out as opposed to going it alone.

Recovery Tasks (5 Minutes)

The following are the recommended recovery tasks for this topic:

Meetings

Encourage the client to (start or) continue going to meetings.

TREATMENT NOTE

Variety

Check to see whether the client is attending different meetings with as wide a range of Al-Anon or Nar-Anon members as possible, including newcomers and old-timers. Encourage the client to begin to look for one or two people (of the same sex as themselves) who have been involved in Al-Anon or Nar-Anon for at least two years and who impress him or her as having learned to face alcoholism successfully. This will be used soon to help the client select a temporary sponsor if she or he does not get one spontaneously.

Telephone and Internet Therapy

Continue to encourage the client to take advantage of the telephone, texting, and e-mail to develop a network of Al-Anon or Nar-Anon friends. These friends will come in handy if and when a crisis occurs. Remind the client, "When you need a friend, you don't want to be calling a stranger."

Readings

Provide the client with Topic 6: Handout 2, Reading Assignments. Review the handout for these suggested readings:

> *Al-Anon Faces Alcoholism*, pages 113–16: "I Belong to Something"; pages 180–86: "A Mother of a Teenaged Alcoholic"[2]

Encourage the client to read other Al-Anon stories of his or her choice and to share them with you.

Journal and Handouts

Remind the client to keep making use of the journal to record thoughts and reactions and responses to handouts for later discussion if she or he has been doing so. It is not too late for the client to start journaling now, if she or he hasn't done so before. Provide Topic 6: Handout 3, Journaling Possibility: Unmanageability, to the client in case he or she wants to further explore (and later discuss) this topic.

Caring Detachment

Working collaboratively with the client, come up with one or two specific ideas for things that she or he can do to begin to decrease enabling the substance abuser and increase caring detachment.

Chapter 13 || Caring Detachment versus Enabling

Topic 7: Caring Detachment

The subject of this session is caring detachment. Analogous to sobriety in substance abusers, caring detachment can be thought of as a primary goal for significant others. Although working on detaching has been a focus throughout the FRP, in this session, the therapist pays special attention to identifying any issues that stand in the way of the significant other relating to the substance abuser in this way.

Review (10–15 Minutes)

The therapist should begin this session, like prior sessions, with a discussion of the client's experiences since the last meeting. As usual, briefly touch on each of the following areas:

Journal and Handouts

Did the client maintain a journal or respond to anything contained in the handouts? If so, are there any entries or responses that she or he would like you to read (or would like to read to you)? Take a few minutes to discuss any such journal entries or responses, and encourage the client to continue writing.

Readings

Did the client follow up on the suggested readings? What reactions or questions does she or he have?

Meetings

How many Al-Anon or Nar-Anon meetings did the client attend? At this point, has he or she begun to bond with the fellowship? If not, what might be standing in the way of the bonding process?

Does the client have any reservations at this point about continuing to attend Al-Anon or Nar-Anon meetings? Can these be worked through in any way?

Telephone and Internet Therapy

Has the client accepted and used any phone numbers? Is there anything that can be done to facilitate this?

Caring Detachment

What progress has the client made since the last session to start or continue the process of relating to the substance abuser through caring detachment? How has his or her behavior changed in relation to the substance abuser? What has his or her level of comfort been in making these changes?

What reaction, if any, has the substance abuser had to these changes on the part of the client?

New Material (30 Minutes)

Detaching can be thought of as the opposite of enabling. It is very different, however, from either alienation or rejection of the substance abuser. Caring detachment is, in fact, very loving. It can also be thought of as the opposite of unhealthy dependency, in that a *relationship based on mutual caring detachment could be characterized as interdependent, as opposed to the dependency that addiction creates.* Caring detachment is a quality found in a relationship between equals (i.e., adult to adult), in contrast to the typical substance abuser–codependent dynamic, which parallels that of child to adult. It is based on mutual support and respect, which allows both partners the dignity of their choices.

As addiction progresses, significant others—especially spouses—become increasingly burdened by feelings of responsibility for their substance abusers. Slowly but surely, many move into a parental role; meanwhile, the substance abuser regresses toward a more infantile state. The burden the codependent carries gradually takes its toll on his or her physical, psychological, and spiritual health.

The goal in recovery for the codependent is to make gradual changes in the way she or he relates to the substance abuser to move the relationship back to the level of adult-to-adult. Doing so leads to improved self-esteem and mental health for codependents. Practicing caring detachment can relieve codependents of much of the burden of shame and guilt that is often the ultimate result of their unsuccessful efforts to control the substance abusers. It can also provide relief from the feelings of rejection and low self-esteem associated with losing a loved one to addiction. Lastly, although that is not its primary intent, in the long run, caring detachment frequently motivates the substance abuser to consider changing.

The following quote from *One Day at a Time in Al-Anon* can be used as the starting point for a discussion of caring detachment:

> "Detach!" we are told in Al-Anon. This does not mean detaching ourselves, and our love and compassion, from the alcoholic. Detachment, in the Al-Anon sense, means to realize we are individuals. We are not bound morally to shoulder the alcoholic's responsibilities.[1]

Ask the client to describe to you what his or her idea of enabling is and then to contrast enabling with caring detachment. Make sure that each of the following points are covered at some point in this discussion:

- Enabling and caring detachment refer to different ways of relating to the substance abuser.
- Caring detachment can be thought of as the opposite of enabling. Whereas enabling protects or cushions the alcoholic or addict from the natural consequences of substance abuse and preserves the status quo in the substance abuser–codependent relationship, detachment, at least in part, means allowing the alcoholic or addict to face those consequences and tends to upset the relational status quo.
- Detachment is based on the idea of each party in a relationship taking responsibility for himself or herself while still feeling love and concern for the other. Another way to think of it is allowing the substance abuser to have the dignity of his or her disease without someone else taking it on.
- The typical substance abuser–codependent relationship is one of parent to child, with the substance abuser's dependency extending beyond an unhealthy dependence on alcohol or other drugs to include an unhealthy dependence on the significant other.

- In the long run, the significant other's inability to contain the addiction process, combined with the experience of losing a loved one to alcohol or other drugs, leads to resentment, shame, and guilt in the significant other and, ultimately, to alienation in the relationship. By moving the substance abuser–codependent relationship from one based on enabling to one based on caring detachment, the significant other can be released from these feelings and begin a process of healing.

Just as it is important to clarify what detachment is, it is important to clarify what it is not. When many loved ones of substance abusers hear the word detachment or hear others in Al-Anon talking about "letting go" or "turning over," they wrongly conclude that they are being urged to reject, leave, or even divorce the substance abuser. This is not the case at all. Caring detachment is based in love, not rejection. One can love someone deeply, yet allow him or her to take responsibility for himself or herself. That is basically what caring detachment is. To achieve it, however (especially after a long-standing pattern of dependency has been established in a relationship) is not easy. To move toward caring detachment, the client needs to be helped to overcome any barriers that stand in the way.

Barriers to Detaching

Detaching makes sense to most people, yet on a practical level, many of these same people find it hard to integrate a detached attitude into their behavior. They shy away from allowing the alcoholic or drug addict to experience and deal with whatever consequences substance use brings his or her way. They continue to relate to the substance abuser as though she or he were a dependent child. Why is this so?

The most common barriers to effective detachment are guilt, anxiety, and misplaced love, all of which usually have one or more of these sources:

- confusing love for someone with responsibility for his or her actions
- believing that allowing the alcoholic or addict to experience negative consequences is somehow unloving or cruel
- believing that it is possible, through love or through plain willpower, to control or change another person's obsession
- feeling that somehow you have caused the addiction
- fearing that not protecting the substance abuser will lead to even greater disaster

Discuss each of these possible barriers to detachment with the client. Guilt that stems from feeling disloyal or cruel can be worked through by acknowledging the positive motives for enabling and by pointing out how enabling is defeating for both the substance abuser and the significant other in the long run, how it actually sets the stage for a substance use problem to get worse instead of better. Check to see whether this is an issue for the client and if so, whether his or her guilt can be relieved by shifting the focus from the short-term benefits to the long-run risks of enabling.

Next, read and discuss the following Al-Anon statement with the client (which is also found at the top of Topic 7: Handout 2, Enabling versus Detaching):

> Learning to detach is a great kindness to ourselves and to the chemically dependent person, and well worth overcoming the obstacles in the beginning. One reward of detachment is that it frees us to grow, to "live and let live."[2]

Confusing love with responsibility is an easy thing to do, but it is dangerous to the present health and future growth of both parties in a relationship. This issue can be approached through a role-reversal technique. Ask the client whether she or he believes someone else should take responsibility for what she or he does or for consequences that result from his or her own actions. Ask if that is a good attitude for parents to take toward their children, for friends to take toward each other, or for spouses to have.

Most people are able see the wisdom in caring detachment, although a few will be troubled by some lingering feeling that it is somehow disloyal or unloving. Some people's idea of love may be very close to what others would call mutual dependency. Even some of those who do see the virtues in detaching, though, may still need a great deal of coaching and support from the therapist and from others in Al-Anon or Nar-Anon in learning to let go of trying to control the substance abuser. By bonding to a Twelve Step fellowship, these codependents can get the caring support, encouragement, and concrete advice they will need over the long run to change the ingrained dynamics of their relationships with the substance abusers.

Holding on to the (sometimes unconscious) belief that "love can cure all" or that one person's willpower can substitute for another's may be the most tenacious form of resistance to detaching. A frank and respectful dialogue around this issue may help a reluctant client put his or her own beliefs in perspective and may set the stage for learning to live and let live, as the preceding statement advocates. It is, after all, not possible for us to substitute our will for someone else's. And even if we could succeed in such a feat, what would that mean for the growth and development of the other person? Most likely, it would stifle any possibility for such growth.

Read Topic 7: Handout 1, Enabling/Detaching Worksheet, with the client. Next, read the sample situation from Topic 7: Handout 2, Enabling versus Detaching (which is also reproduced below) to your client and help him or her identify the enabling and detached responses.

> Sample situation: An alcoholic wakes up hungover and leaves for work more than an hour late for the third time in as many weeks.
>
> Enabling response: The client calls in with an excuse for the alcoholic.
>
> Detached response: The client lets the alcoholic deal with his or her employer, refusing to act as a middleperson.

Give the client Topic 7: Handout 2, Enabling versus Detaching. Help the client to come up with two additional examples of real or imagined situations and then complete the enabling and detached responses. If possible, draw on his or her personal experience with the substance abuser:

Situation 1: ________________________________

Enabling response: ____________________________

Detached response: ____________________________

Situation 2: ________________________________

Enabling response: ____________________________

Detached response: ____________________________

After helping the client complete part 1 of the handout, move on to part 2.

TREATMENT NOTE

The Angry Codependent

The angry father of an alcoholic son once declared, "I'm detached from Michael, alright. I don't ever want to see him again!"

Angry and alienated, significant others can sometimes use the concept of detaching to justify their anger and as a rationale for outright rejection of the addict. Although the client will no doubt find validation for feelings of anger and alienation at Al-Anon or Nar-Anon meetings, she or he will not, in general, find support for using those feelings as a justification for rejection. Similarly, a spouse may find support for an eventual decision to separate from an addict, but not in anger or vengeance. What people will find through Al-Anon and Nar-Anon is support for caring detachment and for taking care of themselves.

Al-Anon and Nar-Anon, like AA and NA, believe that alcoholics are sick people, not bad people. From this perspective, angry rejection is misplaced. Al-Anon and Nar-Anon strongly advocate a "live and let live" attitude in their publications. Instead of rejection, one finds strong support for "turning over" the substance abuser to one's Higher Power while taking care of one's own physical, spiritual, and mental health.

The therapist should approach the issue of a client's pent-up frustration and anger directly, because there is usually a great deal of pain underlying such feelings. It is important to validate such understandable feelings, as well as feelings of alienation. The therapist can also acknowledge that some substance abuser–codependent relationships eventually end in divorce or loss of contact as a consequence of the substance abuse. At the same time, the therapist should make the point that the Al-Anon and Nar-Anon approach to relationships emphasizes honesty and detachment, but not hatred or vindictiveness. These fellowships recognize the pain and hopelessness that lie beneath the anger and alienation.

The goal for Al-Anon and Nar-Anon members is to stop living the alcoholics' lives and start living their own. The more a significant other is able to do this, the more his or her resentment is likely to subside. Caring detachment, as illustrated earlier, is characterized by certain behaviors, but more deeply, it is based in a system of values and an approach to relationships that emphasize self-respect and dignity. By shifting the focus from the substance abuser to the client, the Twelve Step approach opens the way to emotional healing and renewed personal growth.

Summing Up

Remind the client that in future sessions, you will be interested to hear about progress she or he is making in practicing caring detachment. Specifically, you will be interested in hearing about how he or she has begun to think less about the substance user and more about himself or herself. Similarly, you will be interested in learning what progress he or she has made toward not shielding the substance abuser from the natural consequences of alcohol or drug use.

Suggest that substance abusers usually notice and react to changes in the way others relate to them and that you will be available to talk about this when it happens. However, point out that it will be even more important for the client to discuss it with Al-Anon or Nar-Anon friends. For this reason, having a network of such friends, whom the client sees regularly at meetings and also talks to on the phone, becomes more and more important.

Ask the client to summarize what she or he got out of this session and what changes, if any, she or he needs to work toward in the relationship with the substance abuser.

TREATMENT NOTE

The Progression of Addiction

One needs to appreciate how denial—in the substance abuser and the significant other alike—can be tenacious. It would not be unusual, for example, for a significant other, even at this stage in the program and in the face of overwhelming evidence to the contrary, to persist in the belief that his or her loved one can somehow control his or her use of alcohol or other drugs. As one wife put it, "In my head, I tell myself he's an alcoholic and an addict, but another part of me still wants to know why he just can't give up the drugs and have just a couple of beers now and then." As evidence in support of her belief, she cited the fact that her husband was able to limit himself to a couple of beers about one-third of the time that he drank. However, the rest of the time, he got completely drunk. And when he used cocaine, he invariably consumed his entire supply, despite his constant intention to save some for later.

The therapist responded to this woman by pointing out there is not a sharp line separating one stage of substance use from another and that, although her husband seemed clearly to be a habitual user, it was not completely clear that he was as yet a compulsive user. In other words, although he had a clear commitment to alcohol and cocaine (one that interfered with his commitments at home and at work), he was not as yet a slave to them. Rather than attempting to argue with this client about how much control her husband still had over his use, the therapist emphasized that addiction was progressive, pointed out how the negative consequences of her husband's drinking and drug abuse had been accruing for several years, becoming a major problem, and gently reminded the client that she had not been successful at initiating any significant change, much less a halt, in the process so far.

The wife agreed that what the therapist said made sense. She continued going to both Al-Anon and Nar-Anon meetings. In time, she got a sponsor and continued the process of caring detachment that had begun to elicit some definite reactions from her husband.

If resistance to Step One (acceptance of loss of control over alcohol or drug use) is evident at all at this point in FRP treatment, it can be useful for the therapist to check again as to what the client thinks about the substance abuser's stage of use and to compare it to what the client thought when the assessment was first done, especially in light of any new information that has emerged in the course of treatment.

Recovery Tasks (5 Minutes)

The following are the suggested recovery tasks for this topic:

Meetings

Ask the client to continue to attend two or three Al-Anon or Nar-Anon meetings per week and to journal about his or her reactions. Remind the client about the importance of building a network of Al-Anon or Nar-Anon friends and to nurture that network through phone and e-mail contacts. The purpose of this, again, is simple: The therapist will not always be there, and it is much better to call a friend than a stranger when a crisis occurs.

Sponsorship

Ask the client to begin talking to other Al-Anon or Nar-Anon members about sponsorship. By now, some clients may have already bonded to the fellowship and selected a sponsor. If this is so, the therapist merely needs to reinforce this move toward bonding with the fellowship and inquire briefly how the client selected this person as a sponsor and what this relationship is like: how often they talk, what the sponsor advises, and so forth.

If the client has not yet selected a sponsor, explain that one goal of the FRP is to help him or her select a temporary sponsor and that you will be discussing this more in the next session. Between now and then, though, the client should give some thought to which Al-Anon or Nar-Anon members he or she most respects, who have had experiences at least somewhat similar to his or her own, and who might be potential sponsors.

Readings

Provide the client with Topic 7: Handout 3, Reading Assignments, and review the recommended readings for this topic:

> *Al-Anon Faces Alcoholism*, pages 31–36: "Detachment and Growth"; pages 255–57: "Other Tools of the Program—Sponsorship"[3]
>
> Al-Anon pamphlet *So You Love an Alcoholic*[4]
>
> Caroline W., *Detaching with Love*[5]

Journal and Handouts

Provide the client with Topic 7: Handout 4, Journaling Possibility: Enabling versus Caring Detachment, and Handout 5, Journaling Possibility: Barriers to Caring Detachment, in case he or she wants to further explore these topics in his or her journal.

Caring Detachment

In collaboration with the client, the therapist should suggest one or two specific things that she or he can do to decrease his or her enabling of the substance abuser and increase caring detachment.

Chapter 14 || Exploring the Concept of Surrender

Topic 8: Surrender

In this session, the therapist focuses on Steps Two and Three of Al-Anon and Nar-Anon and the concept of *surrender.* Key issues for discussion include the notion of "working" the Al-Anon and Nar-Anon Twelve Step program and "turning over" the fate of the substance abuser to a Higher Power: permitting the natural consequences of substance abuse to occur without interference from the significant other, and allowing the substance abuser to make his or her own choices. Instead of focusing on the addict, the significant other begins to focus instead on his or her own well-being.

To make this profound shift, the significant other must have (or be able to find) the faith that this is the best course of action in the long run. The source of this faith may be spiritual; alternately, significant others may elect to place their faith in the collective wisdom of Al-Anon and Nar-Anon and in those peers who have made progress in recovering from codependence. This shift is what is meant by the term *surrender.*

Whatever the source of one's faith, faith is clearly necessary if one is to have the courage to surrender. That surrender, in turn, opens the way to change for the significant other and, indirectly, for the substance abuser as well as a result of changes in the substance abuser–codependent relationship. Surrender, when it is achieved, often leads to a profound sense of relief in significant others. The burden of guilt and shame that many loved ones of substance abusers carry is lifted from them through surrender. Some have likened surrender to a spiritual awakening.

Review (10–15 Minutes)

Begin the session by checking in with the client with respect to his or her experiences since the last session. Be sure to briefly review each of the following areas, all of which have repeatedly been the subjects of recovery tasks:

Journal and Handouts

Did the client maintain a journal or respond to anything contained in the handouts? If so, are there any entries or responses that she or he would like you to read (or would like to read to you)? Take a few minutes to discuss any such journal entries or responses, and encourage the client to continue writing.

Readings

Has the client read any Al-Anon or Nar-Anon literature? What reactions or questions does she or he have? Did the client read either the Hazelden pamphlet *Detaching with Love* or the Al-Anon pamphlet *So You Love an Alcoholic?*[1] What reactions did she or he have to these readings?

Meetings

How many Al-Anon or Nar-Anon meetings did the client attend? Does the client have any reservations at this point about continuing to attend Al-Anon or Nar-Anon meetings? Can these be worked through in any way?

Telephone and Internet Therapy

Has the client been making any telephone or e-mail contacts? How has that been going?

If the client has not made much progress in building a network of contacts, can this be facilitated in any way at this point, for example, through role-playing around any identified barriers?

Sponsorship

Has the client made any progress toward getting a sponsor?

If yes, does the client have regular contact with the sponsor? In general, does she or he seem to respect this person? Most important, would she or he be likely to follow the sponsor's advice in a time of crisis?

TREATMENT NOTE

Facilitating Sponsorship

Getting a sponsor and developing a relationship with that person has been found to correlate with success in recovery from addiction,[2] and it is probably equally important for a significant other's efforts to move toward caring detachment. If the client has still not approached a sponsor at this point in this program, explore this issue once again. Try to identify and, if possible, work through resistance to initiating contact with a sponsor. The following questions may be useful in such a discussion:

- What kind of person would you want to have as a sponsor?
- What could you stand to gain from a relationship with a sponsor?
- Are you willing to give sponsorship a try, say for six months?
- What could we do together to make it possible for you to take that first step to say at a meeting that you're looking for a sponsor or to ask someone if he or she would think about sponsoring you?

TREATMENT NOTE

Assessing the Client's Commitment to Fellowship

By this time it is hoped the client has attended a number of Al-Anon or Nar-Anon meetings and could be said to have at least been exposed to a Twelve Step fellowship. However, the goal here is to go beyond mere exposure and to facilitate the client's *bonding* to an Al-Anon or Nar-Anon group.

It can be useful for the therapist to take some time now to explore with the client the extent to which this goal of bonding has been achieved, using open-ended questions, such as the following:

- How would you describe your reaction to the Al-Anon or Nar-Anon meetings you have attended so far?
- What have you found most useful about meetings? What has been least useful to you?
- Who have you been able to identify with? In what ways can you identify with this person (or persons)?
- Do you look forward to meetings? Do you think you would continue to go to meetings if I weren't specifically asking you to go?

- Do you feel connected to any one Al-Anon or Nar-Anon group, as though you belong there and being there is important to you? If not, what seems to be the stumbling block?
- Do you feel you have a good understanding of the concepts of enabling and caring detachment at this point? Do you have any questions about them?

New Material (30 Minutes)

Surrender

At Al-Anon and Nar-Anon meetings, it is common to hear members urge one another to "turn over" the addict or alcoholic. Such statements refer to the concept of surrender, which derives from the Second and Third Steps of the Twelve Steps.

Behaviorally, surrender has to do with a willingness to stop relating to the substance abuser in ways that shield him or her from the natural consequences of substance abuse and that serve to maintain the status quo in the substance abuser–codependent relationship. Surrender means accepting the need to let the substance abuser face life straight on, including taking responsibility for making choices between continuing substance abuse (and its consequences) or recovery.

Spiritually, surrender challenges significant others to have faith that allowing the substance abuser to find his or her own way is truly the best course of action in the long run—for the addict, for the significant other, and for their relationship. *By surrendering, the client relieves himself or herself of responsibility, first for causing and now for curing the addiction. The codependent is free to take care of his or her own needs.*

As mentioned in previous chapters, by enabling substance abusers (in most cases, for years), significant others unwittingly work to shield the substance abuser and preserve a status quo in the substance abuser–codependent relationship that, ironically, is conducive to maintaining addiction. Many codependents can readily see this, yet the idea of letting go and allowing the substance abuser to experience the natural consequences of substance abuse is fraught with anxieties. For many, the prospect of detaching—the notion of turning over the substance abuser to his or her fate, unfettered, as it were—requires an enormous leap of faith. That is where the Second and Third Steps become particularly relevant for many significant others' struggles to alter their relationships with the substance abusers. These Steps state the following:

Came to believe that a Power greater than ourselves could restore us to sanity.

Made a decision to turn our will and our lives over to the care of God *as we understood Him*.[3]

For some, the ideas expressed in Steps Two and Three will pose little or no problem for significant others. For one thing, they may already believe in a Higher Power of some sort to whom they turn for comfort and whom they can turn to again as they begin to detach and turn over the alcoholic or addict. For another thing, they may have bonded to Al-Anon or Nar-Anon and be willing to turn to others as their Higher Power for support as they detach.

In exploring surrender, it can be helpful to ask the client whether she or he believes in a God and, if so, if she or he ever prays. In other words, is prayer a source of comfort for the client? Is it something that he or she could turn to now as he or she contemplates detaching from the substance abuser? Many clients can relate to the slogan, "Let go and let God," which implies replacing their own willpower with faith in a Higher Power to lead the substance abuser toward recovery. "Letting go and letting God" frees up the significant other to take care of his or her own needs while changing the way he or she relates to the substance abuser in a fundamental way—moving the relationship from one based on guilt and dependency toward one based on mutual respect and interdependence. Faced with such a profound change in his or her relationship with the enabler, many a substance abuser has eventually made a decision to change and to embrace the Twelve Step program of AA and NA as a basis for recovery.

TREATMENT NOTE

Discussing Personal Spiritual Beliefs

Steps Two and Three may tempt the therapist to discuss the client's personal religious beliefs. The issue of spirituality has been brought up earlier, and you may want to review that material again prior to bringing up this topic now. Keep in mind that, although as a therapist you are no doubt a skilled mental health professional, you may not be skilled, trained, or experienced in discussing spiritual issues. Moreover, some therapists may be uncomfortable revealing their personal spiritual beliefs, whereas others may be uncomfortable with certain beliefs. It is sufficient for the therapist to simply point out that Twelve Step fellowships are nonspecific in their advocacy of spiritual belief (i.e., they do not define any particular Higher Power that one is asked to believe in). And as has been stated before, it is entirely appropriate to make the fellowship itself (Al-Anon or Nar-Anon) one's Higher Power.

Clients who reject any concept of God, prayer, or both are not to be criticized, much less subjected to any effort on the part of the therapist to change their beliefs. These persons are as capable of surrender as any religious or spiritual person. They merely need to find some form of support in their efforts to detach.

Slogans

"Turn it over," "Let go and let God," "Came to believe," and "One day at a time"—these are some of the sayings the newcomer to a Twelve Step fellowship is likely to hear repeatedly in meetings. In one way or another, they all relate back to the idea of surrender. They are more than pithy sayings or bumper sticker psychology. They represent a succinct way of keeping the message of Al-Anon and Nar-Anon clear and keeping the goal of caring detachment in focus.

Surrender may seem like a simple concept, but it is no simple task. As any parent who has let go of a child as he or she became an adult can attest, surrender is not always easy. So it is with letting go of a substance abuser whose judgment and capacity for making decisions seems to be clearly impaired.

Slogans support surrender. Many are statements of spiritual faith, as when an Al-Anon or Nar-Anon member speaks of "letting go and letting God." By this slogan, they mean that instead of the significant other, a Higher Power will now assume responsibility for the substance abuser. Such statements of faith can help a great deal when a spouse or other loved one is faced with the challenge of breaking long-standing and entrenched patterns of protecting the substance abuser and taking responsibility for him or her.

"Turning it over" can be taken not only as a statement of spiritual faith, but also as a statement of practical wisdom regarding the limits of any adult's responsibility for the decisions and behavior of another. It is common wisdom within Al-Anon and Nar-Anon that codependents tend to feel overly responsible for their partners' substance use. They believe on some level that either they caused (or at least contributed to) the problem or that they can somehow resolve it. Most harbor underlying fears that detaching will lead to disaster. The long-term impact of their belief that they somehow either caused or else can cure the problems—especially as their efforts repeatedly fail—include all the symptoms associated with depression: fatigue, hopelessness, low self-esteem, declining health, and so on.

Since their inception, Al-Anon and Nar-Anon have recognized the personal devastation associated with codependence. In their wisdom, these fellowships also recognize just how difficult it can be for people to let go of trying to control addiction in a loved one. They are guided by a strong tradition of providing support for members as they gradually turn over the fate of the substance abusers in the belief that this is the best course of action and, ultimately, a loving thing to do.

Assessing Progress

The therapist should now take some time to explore how the client relates to slogans such as those cited earlier and also to assess how much progress is being made thus far toward turning over the alcoholic or addict to a Higher Power—for example, by not interfering with the natural consequences of his or her substance abuse. Use the foregoing material and Topic 8: Handout 1, Exploring Surrender, as a guideline for discussion. Ask open-ended questions such as the following:

- Have you heard the expression "Turn it over?" How about "Let go and let God?" or "Came to believe?" What do these expressions mean to you, in terms of your relationship with ______(insert name)______?
- What do you think you would need to do, concretely, to feel okay about turning it over, in the sense of allowing him or her to be responsible for his or her own actions and their consequences and trusting that this is the best thing you can do for both of you?
- What internal resistance do you think you still have to turning over ____________'s substance use problem in the way just stated? For example, would you feel anxious? Guilty?

Walking the Walk

To members of Twelve Step fellowships, the expression "walking the walk" is a familiar and highly meaningful one. In the area of psychotherapy, this same concept has been written about using the more technical phrase, *surrender versus compliance in therapy.*[4] In either case, the basic concept is the same and has to do with the extent to which the individual is committed to a program of recovery and bonded to Al-Anon or Nar-Anon or is merely attending meetings. The latter could be called passive involvement and is associated with what is called "talking the talk." The former alternative—commitment and bonding—reflects true active involvement. This is what "walking the walk" means.

From the perspective of those who truly walk the walk of recovery, the merely compliant individual—one who may attend Al-Anon meetings but who does not participate actively in the fellowship—is not likely to surrender or to experience the maximum benefits that commitment offers. Compliant individuals may go to meetings, but they don't open up, don't develop a network of contacts, don't get a sponsor, don't volunteer for service work, and so forth. In a word, they don't bond. As a result, they may also have difficulty giving up their enabling behaviors and attitudes, because they will lack the ongoing support to do so and the faith in the wisdom and effectiveness of caring detachment.

"Talking the talk," in Twelve Step terms, is the opposite of "walking the walk." Often it amounts to little more than going through the motions, perhaps to placate you, the therapist. It is, in a word, mere compliance. If this is the case, then it is reasonable to expect that the client will revert to old ways of relating to the substance abuser once treatment is terminated.

Initially, the therapist asked nothing more of the client than to give Al-Anon or Nar-Anon a try. Now is an appropriate time to press the issue of whether the client is ready and willing to move beyond mere compliance—beyond talking the talk—to the level of commitment to Al-Anon or Nar-Anon as a vehicle for personal growth, as a viable way of coping with the formidable task of being in a relationship with an addict, and for moving the substance abuser–codependent relationship in a healthier direction. In short, is he or she ready to walk the walk?

Surrender involves a willingness to become truly active and involved in Al-Anon or Nar-Anon, as opposed to merely looking in from the outside, as one significant other put it. The therapist should make this distinction clear and then ask the client to think about how much she or he is willing to trust Al-Anon or Nar-Anon, to adopt its philosophy, and to embrace the Twelve Step program as a pathway to recovery for himself or herself. Toward this end, the therapist might provide the client with Topic 8: Handout 2, Walking the Walk, and ask the client the following questions:

- How committed are you at this point to regularly attending Al-Anon or Nar-Anon meetings: not at all, somewhat, or very committed?
- Do you make use of Al-Anon or Nar-Anon literature in helping you to learn to detach?
- Do you cultivate a network of Al-Anon or Nar-Anon friends whom you talk to regularly? How do you do this?

Sponsorship

Another step toward commitment and bonding comes when the significant other gets a sponsor and communicates regularly with that person. If the client has not as yet found a sponsor, address the issue again, now in the context of this idea of surrender. Using the expression, "Walking the walk," ask whether the client is now willing to pursue the matter of selecting a temporary Al-Anon or Nar-Anon sponsor. If necessary, clarify again the following regarding the role of the sponsor:

- Sponsors should be individuals of the same sex as the client and who have been active in Al-Anon or Nar-Anon for a minimum of one year.
- Sponsors have sponsors of their own.
- Sponsors are not therapists and do not pretend to be.
- Sponsors offer sound advice about how to work the Twelve Steps of Al-Anon and Nar-Anon and how to move from enabling toward caring detachment.
- Sponsees should expect to be in frequent contact with their sponsors, either in person, via phone, or via e-mail.

Surrender and Release

So far, this session has focused mostly on some of the cognitive and behavioral facets of surrender. What has been mentioned but not fully explored as yet is the emotional impact associated with surrender.

It has been pointed out that the loved ones of addicts and alcoholics, be they parents, spouses, or siblings, often carry a burden of guilt and shame. Many feel, on some level, that they somehow caused or at least contributed to the substance abuse problem. They feel shame that this disease has been cast on them. Wives in particular are apt to feel these things, because our society continues to place the major responsibility for relationships on women.

As addiction progresses and the relationship between the loved one and the substance abuser gives way to the substance abuser's relationship with alcohol or drugs, jealousy leads to resentment and eventually to alienation and low self-esteem in the significant other. The spiritual well-being of codependents, including their outlook on life, their approach to relationships, and their faith, declines steadily as addiction progresses, leaving them physically, emotionally, and spiritually drained.

Surrender, like caring detachment, is something that is best approached as a process. However, at some point, many significant others report an experience not unlike a spiritual awakening. This appears to come when they have the clear realization that they can and should let go of their old way of relating to the substance abuser. Associated with this realization is a profound sense of release: release from guilt and shame, to be sure, but also from the stress and anxiety that come from being chronically vigilant, trying to protect a substance abuser from the consequences of his or her decisions, and trying to substitute one's own will for that of another.

The sense of relief that comes from letting go of guilt and responsibility for someone else's decisions and behavior and instead feeling free to begin to focus on one's own needs is powerful indeed. It has been described using terms ranging from the relatively mild—*invigorating*—to words that conjure up images of a profound shift in perception of self and others. Hearing people relate such experiences helps one appreciate more fully the Twelfth and last Step of the Twelve Step program: "Having had a spiritual awakening as the result of these steps, we tried to carry this message to alcoholics [codependents], and to practice these principles in all our affairs."[5]

Summing Up

The therapist should once more take a couple of minutes to ask the client to summarize, in his or her own words, what he or she has gotten out of this session. Particular attention should be paid to gaining the client's honest response to how willing he or she is at this time to commit to Al-Anon or Nar-Anon and the Twelve Step program. Reluctance to totally commit should not be challenged; rather, clarify the client's reasons for this. Keep in mind that thus far you have primarily asked the client only to give Al-Anon or Nar-

Anon a try and now you are pressing for a greater commitment. The client may indeed need some time to stop and think about this.

Recovery Tasks (5 Minutes)

Suggested recovery tasks for this topic are as follows:

Meetings

Continue to specifically encourage and reinforce attendance at Al-Anon or Nar-Anon meetings or both. Be sure to ask how connected the client feels to certain Al-Anon or Nar-Anon groups and members and whether she or he has decided on a home meeting yet. If the client says that she or he does not yet feel connected, suggest that she or he continue going to meetings with the agenda of listening and trying to identify with at least parts of others' experiences, because identification is where bonding begins.

Readings

Provide the client with Topic 8: Handout 3, Reading Assignments, and review the recommended reading for this topic:

> *Al-Anon Faces Alcoholism*, pages 125–28: "A Return to Faith by Way of Al-Anon"[6]

Caring Detachment

As in previous sessions, end by working collaboratively with the client to come up with one or two specific things he or she can do to begin to decrease enabling of the substance abuser and increase caring detachment.

Program Assessment

In preparation for the next (and final) session, the therapist may want to duplicate and provide the client with Topic 8: Handout 4, Program Assessment. Request that the client complete this program assessment in advance of your next session, so you can more effectively discuss the program with him or her.

Chapter 15 || Termination

The termination session of this program, like the introductory session, has its own unique format. The primary goal of this final session is to allow the therapist and client, together, to process the client's experiences in the program. A second goal is to assess the client's plans for future action. The therapist, of course, encourages continuing involvement in Al-Anon or Nar-Anon. However, any movement on the part of the client toward caring detachment, as well as for taking better care of his or her own needs, is to be commended.

TREATMENT NOTE

On Client-Therapist Bonding

Clinical experience with the FRP suggests that some clients may become quite bonded to the therapist over time. This is understandable, of course, and happens frequently in any counseling relationship. It is more likely to happen here if the client has made less use of Al-Anon or Nar-Anon than of the therapist in his or her efforts to detach from the substance abuser. The experienced therapist will have anticipated this, will have perceived this bonding as it progressed, and will have brought it—and the reasons for it—into the open for discussion.

A major rationale for systematically encouraging Al-Anon or Nar-Anon involvement throughout this program, of course, has been to reduce reliance on the therapist and increase reliance on a Twelve Step fellowship for support and advice. Still, despite such efforts, some clients may, in fact, feel dependent on the therapist for their continued recovery.

Though many clients accept the reality of termination with equanimity, it is not that unusual for a client to ask to continue to see the therapist and sometimes to express considerable anxiety about termination. If this happens, it is recommended that the therapist offer the client any one of the following options:

- to be available to the client *occasionally* via telephone or e-mail (but not regularly, and not for the purpose of extended one-to-one counseling)

- to offer a "booster session" one month following termination
- to offer a follow-up of a few (two or three) additional sessions six months after termination

The rationale for offering only these options is to encourage the client to use and bond with Al-Anon or Nar-Anon (as opposed to the therapist) as his or her primary resource for recovery. At the same time these suggestions recognize the validity of the client-therapist relationship as a force for change.

Program Assessment

In all likelihood, different clients will have found different parts of this program more or less helpful. Recognizing this fact and sharing that expectation with the client at the outset of this last session will encourage honesty in giving feedback to the therapist. The following is presented as a guideline for helping significant others evaluate their experiences in this program. The therapist should be careful not to rush through this material and might even take notes of the client's comments.

Attitudes toward Alcoholism and Addiction

- Does the client now believe that he or she can somehow control his or her loved one's use of alcohol or other drugs?
- At this point, does the client feel responsible in any way for causing his or her loved one's substance use?
- How does the client understand the concept of denial as it applies to the substance abuser? How does he or she understand it as it applies to himself or herself?
- How has the client enabled the substance abuser?
- What is the client's understanding of caring detachment? What progress, if any, has he or she made in moving from enabling toward detaching?

Attitudes toward Al-Anon or Nar-Anon

What was the client's view of Al-Anon or Nar-Anon prior to treatment? What is it now?

What has been the client's experience with each of the following with respect to their helpfulness?

- going to meetings
- getting a sponsor
- readings
- telephone and Internet therapy
- establishing a network of Al-Anon or Nar-Anon friends
- sponsorship
- journaling
- handouts

Next, inquire about the client's thoughts in each of the following areas:

- Based on his or her experience, would the client recommend Al-Anon or Nar-Anon to a friend who confided that he or she had a loved one who had an alcohol or other drug problem?
- What are the client's plans regarding Al-Anon or Nar-Anon involvement for the immediate future?

Attitudes toward the Family Recovery Program (FRP)

Feedback from the client about what he or she found most and least useful about his or her experience with this program provides an opportunity for the therapist to continually enhance his or her clinical expertise. Ask the client for his or her thoughts on each of the following:

- What were the most useful parts of this treatment program?
- What were the least useful parts of this program?
- What is the most important idea or ideas that the client gained from these sessions?
- If the client could change any part of this program, what would that change be?
- Would the client recommend this program to other significant others of substance abusers? What would he or she say about it to such persons?

It is hoped that a thorough and frank discussion of questions like the preceding will leave both the therapist and the client with an appreciation for the work they have done collaboratively during the course of these sessions and with a sense of where the client will go from here.

Summing Up

This treatment experience would not be complete if the therapist did not finish it by asking the client for his or her bottom-line assessment:

- How are you different now than you were when we first met?
- How is your relationship different now than it was at the start of this program?
- If change has occurred in your relationship, to what do you attribute that change?
- If things have not changed since you began this program, could that be because the status quo in your relationship with the substance abuser has not changed? If that is the case, what would it take to change the status quo between you and the substance abuser in ways that would free you to become healthier and happier while letting the substance abuser take more responsibility for himself or herself?

Parting

Although not typically done in psychotherapy, it is not inappropriate in this kind of intervention for the therapist and the client to exchange tokens of regard for one another as well as to commemorate the start of the client's recovery, if they choose to do so. Appropriate mementos include Al-Anon or Nar-Anon medallions, greeting cards, meditation books, and so forth. These are readily available today through bookstores. If the therapist and the client elect to part in such a manner, this should of course be discussed and planned in advance.

Whether they choose to celebrate the end of the Family Recovery Program with some ritual, though, it is important to part on good terms. Recovery, for codependents and substance abusers alike, is much like the proverbial journey that is taken a single step at a time. The very fact that the significant other has chosen to complete the FRP represents one such step.

II Forms and Handouts on the CD-ROM

Session Guidelines Overview

Topic 1: Introduction and Assessment

Session Guidelines
Handout 1: Relational Model of Addiction
Handout 2: Progression of Substance Use
Handout 3: Inventory of Negative Consequences
Handout 4: Reading Assignments
Handout 5: Journaling Possibility: Reflections about Resentment and Shame

Topic 2: The Principles of Twelve Step Fellowships

Session Guidelines
Handout 1: Readings
Handout 2: Three Questions to Ask Yourself
Handout 3: Spirituality
Handout 4: Reading Assignments

Topic 3: Al-Anon and Nar-Anon

Session Guidelines
Handout 1: Four Questions to Ask Yourself
Handout 2: Reading Assignments
Handout 3: Journaling Possibility: Describing Your Higher Power

Topic 4: Denial

Session Guidelines
Handout 1: Discussing Powerlessness
Handout 2: The Seven Forms of Denial
Handout 3: Writing Exercises
Handout 4: Questions on Denial

Topic 5: Enabling

Topic 6: Acceptance

Topic 7: Caring Detachment

Topic 8: Surrender

Termination

Suggested Reading

Al-Anon Faces Alcoholism. 2nd ed. New York: Al-Anon Family Group Headquarters, 1989.

Alcoholics Anonymous. 4th ed. New York: Alcoholics Anonymous World Services, 2001.

Am I an Addict? Van Nuys, CA: Narcotics Anonymous World Services, 1983.

Narcotics Anonymous. 6th ed. Van Nuys, CA: Narcotics Anonymous World Services, 2008.

So You Love an Alcoholic. Midtown Station, NY: Al-Anon Family Group Headquarters, n.d.

Twelve Steps and Twelve Traditions. New York: Alcoholics Anonymous World Services, 2002.

Understanding Ourselves and Alcoholism. New York: Al-Anon Family Group Headquarters, 1979.

W., Carolyn. *Detaching with Love*. Revised ed. Center City, MN: Hazelden, 1994.

Notes

Preface to the Second Edition

1. J. E. James and M. Goldman, "Behavior Trends in Wives of Alcoholics," *Quarterly Journal of Studies on Alcoholism* 32 (1971): 373–81.

2. E. J. Thomas and R. D. Ager, "Characteristics of Unmotivated Alcohol Abusers and Their Spouses" (paper presented at the Research Society on Alcoholism, Annual Meeting, San Antonio, Texas, June 1993).

3. T. P. Dominguez, W. R. Miller, and R. J. Meyers, "Unilateral Intervention with Family Members of Problem Drinkers" (Albuquerque: University of New Mexico, Center for Alcoholism, Substance Abuse, and Addictions, unpublished paper, 1995).

4. R. L. Collins, K. E. Leonard, and J. S. Searles, *Alcohol and the Family: Research and Clinical Perspectives* (New York: Guilford, 1990); T. J. Paolino and B. S. McCrady, *The Alcoholic Marriage: Alternative Perspectives* (New York: Grune and Stratton, 1977).

5. M. G. Snow, J. O. Prochaska, and J. S. Rossi, "Stages of Change for Smoking-Cessation among Former Problem Drinkers: A Cross-Sectional Analysis," *Journal of Substance Abuse* 4 (1992): 107–16.

6. W. R. Miller and R. J. Meyers, "Clinical Trial of Interventions with Significant Others," NIAAA Grant No. R01AA09774-01A1 (Albuquerque: University of New Mexico, Center for Alcoholism, Substance Abuse, and Addictions, 1994); W. R. Miller and R. J. Meyers, "Unilateral Family Intervention for Drug Problems: Stage Two Trial," NIDA Grant No. R01DA08896-01 (Albuquerque: University of New Mexico, Center for Alcoholism, Substance Abuse, and Addictions, 1996).

Part 1

Chapter 1

1. The terms *concerned significant other* and *codependent* are used in this text more or less interchangeably. They refer to any loved one of a substance abuser who has been affected as a result of being in a relationship with that substance abuser. The use of the term *codependent* is not intended to be pejorative in any way. The phrase *concerned significant other* could have been used exclusively but seemed unwieldy. The term *codependent* does imply some effect of addiction on loved ones, and this is, in fact, what Twelve Step fellowships assume to be the case. Moreover, the term is commonly used within Twelve Step fellowships. The author does not, however, wish to endorse any definition of *codependence* other than what is described herein (i.e., to be in a

close relationship with a substance abuser and to therefore be affected by addiction). The term as used herein is generic and is not intended to imply any specific psychopathology. Similarly, the term *client* is used here to refer to a concerned significant other of a substance abuser.

2. J. O. Prochaska, C. C. DiClemente, and J. C. Norcross, "In Search of How People Change: Applications to Addictive Behaviors," *American Psychologist* 47, no. 9 (1992).

3. Alcoholics Anonymous, *Alcoholics Anonymous,* 4th ed. (New York: Alcoholics Anonymous World Services, 2001); Narcotics Anonymous, *Narcotics Anonymous,* 6th ed. (Van Nuys, CA: Narcotics Anonymous World Services, 2008).

4. Alcoholics Anonymous, *Alcoholics Anonymous,* 4th ed., 104–21.

5. Alcoholics Anonymous, *Alcoholics Anonymous,* 4th ed., 108–9.

6. Alcoholics Anonymous, *Alcoholics Anonymous,* 4th ed., 109.

7. Alcoholics Anonymous, *Alcoholics Anonymous,* 4th ed., 110.

8. J. W. Fowler, "Alcoholics Anonymous and Faith Development," in *Research on Alcoholics Anonymous: Opportunities and Alternatives,* ed. B. S. McCrady and W. R. Miller (New Brunswick, NJ: Rutgers University, 1993), 113–35.

9. R. Room, "Alcoholics Anonymous as a Social Movement," in *Research on Alcoholics Anonymous: Opportunities and Alternatives,* ed. B. S. McCrady and W. R. Miller (New Brunswick, NJ: Rutgers University Press, 1993), 119–31.

10. Alcoholics Anonymous, *Alcoholics Anonymous,* 4th ed., 62.

11. Al-Anon, *Al-Anon Faces Alcoholism*, 2nd ed. (New York: Al-Anon Family Group Headquarters, 1989).

12. Al-Anon, *Al-Anon Faces Alcoholism*, 2nd ed., 236.

13. Al-Anon, *Al-Anon Faces Alcoholism*, 2nd ed., 236.

14. Al-Anon, *Al-Anon Faces Alcoholism*, 2nd ed., 232, 236.

15. Al-Anon, *Al-Anon Faces Alcoholism*, 2nd ed., 29.

16. Narcotics Anonymous, *Narcotics Anonymous,* 6th ed., 21.

17. Alcoholics Anonymous, *Alcoholics Anonymous,* 4th ed., 104–21.

18. Alcoholics Anonymous, *Alcoholics Anonymous,* 4th ed., 107.

19. Alcoholics Anonymous, *Alcoholics Anonymous,* 4th ed., 120.

20. R. J. Meyers and J. E. Smith, *Clinical Guide to Alcohol Treatment: The Community Reinforcement Approach* (New York: Guilford, 1995).

21. Alcoholics Anonymous, *Alcoholics Anonymous,* 4th ed., 111.

22. Alcoholics Anonymous, *Alcoholics Anonymous,* 4th ed., 113.

23. Alcoholics Anonymous, *Alcoholics Anonymous,* 4th ed., 112.

24. Alcoholics Anonymous, *Alcoholics Anonymous,* 4th ed., 115.

25. J. Nowinski, "Self-Help Groups for Addictions," in *Addictions: A Comprehensive Guidebook for Practitioners,* ed. B. S. McCrady and E. E. Epstein (New York: Oxford University Press, 1999).

26. Al-Anon, *Al-Anon Faces Alcoholism,* 2nd ed.; Alcoholics Anonymous, *Alcoholics Anonymous,* 4th ed.

27. Narcotics Anonymous, *Narcotics Anonymous,* 6th ed.

Chapter 2

1. Al-Anon, *Al-Anon Faces Alcoholism*, 2nd ed. (New York: Al-Anon Family Group Headquarters, 1989), 246–52.

2. G. A. Marlatt, J. A. Tucker, D. M. Donovan, and R. E. Vuchinich, "Help-Seeking by Substance Abusers: The Role of Harm Reduction and Behavioral-Economic Approaches to Facilitate Treatment Entry and Retention," in *Beyond the Therapeutic Alliance: Keeping the Drug-Dependent Individual in Treatment,* ed. L. S. Onken, J. D. Blaine, and J. J. Boren, NIDA Research Monograph 165 (Rockville, MD: US Department of Health and Human Services, 1997), 44–84.

3. Alcoholics Anonymous, *Alcoholics Anonymous,* 4th ed. (New York: Alcoholics Anonymous World Services, 2001), 60.

4. Alcoholics Anonymous, *Alcoholics Anonymous,* 4th ed., 58–59.

Chapter 3

1. Alcoholics Anonymous, *Living Sober: Some Methods A.A. Members Have Used for Not Drinking* (New York: Alcoholics Anonymous World Services, 1975).

2. Alcoholics Anonymous, "To Wives," in *Alcoholics Anonymous,* 4th ed. (New York: Alcoholics Anonymous World Services, 2001), 104–21; Al-Anon, *Al-Anon Faces Alcoholism*, 2nd ed. (New York: Al-Anon Family Group Headquarters, 1989).

Chapter 4

1. Alcoholics Anonymous, *Alcoholics Anonymous,* 4th ed. (New York: Alcoholics Anonymous World Services, 2001), 59.

2. B. S. McCrady and E. E. Epstein, "Theoretical Bases of Family Approaches to Substance Abuse Treatment," in *Treating Substance Abuse: Theory and Technique,* ed. F. Rotgers, D. S. Keller, and J. Morgenstern (New York: Guilford, 1996), 125–45.

3. R. J. Meyers and J. E. Smith, *Clinical Guide to Alcohol Treatment: The Community Reinforcement Approach* (New York: Guilford, 1995); R. J. Meyers, T. P. Dominguez, and J. E. Smith, "Community Reinforcement Training with Concerned Others," in *Sourcebook of Psychological Treatment Manuals for Adult Disorders,* ed. V. B. Van Hasselt and M. Hersen (New York: Plenum, 1996), 102–127.

4. *Family Matters* (video) (Dick Young Productions, 1988).

5. *Al-Anon Faces Alcoholism*, 2nd ed. (New York: Al-Anon Family Group Headquarters, 1989), 29.

6. Carolyn W., *Detaching with Love,* original ed. (Center City, MN: Hazelden, 1984), 7–8.

7. Carolyn W., *Detaching with Love*, original ed., 16.

8. Alcoholics Anonymous, *Alcoholics Anonymous,* 4th ed., 60.

Chapter 5

1. Al-Anon, *Al-Anon Faces Alcoholism*, 2nd ed. (New York: Al-Anon Family Group Headquarters, 1989); Al-Anon, *One Day at a Time in Al-Anon* (New York: Al-Anon Family Group Headquarters, 1990).

2. Al-Anon, *One Day at a Time in Al-Anon*, 206.

3. Alcoholics Anonymous, *Twelve Steps and Twelve Traditions* (New York: Alcoholics Anonymous World Services, 1952).

4. J. W. Fowler, "Alcoholics Anonymous and Faith Development," in *Research on Alcoholics Anonymous: Opportunities and Alternatives,* ed. B. S. McCrady and W. R. Miller (New Brunswick, NJ: Rutgers University, 1993), 115–16.

5. J. W. Fowler, "Alcoholics Anonymous and Faith Development," in *Research on Alcoholics Anonymous: Opportunities and Alternatives*, 116.

6. Alcoholics Anonymous, *Living Sober: Some Methods A.A. Members Have Used for Not Drinking* (New York: Alcoholics Anonymous World Services, 1975).

7. E. Kurtz, *AA: The Story* (New York: HarperCollins, 1988).

Chapter 6

1. R. J. Solberg, *The Dry Drunk Syndrome*, revised ed. (Center City, MN: Hazelden, 1983, 1993).

2. R. J. Solberg, *The Dry Drunk Syndrome*, revised ed., 3.

3. R. J. Solberg, *The Dry Drunk Syndrome*, revised ed., 3–5.

4. R. J. Meyers and J. E. Smith, *Clinical Guide to Alcohol Treatment: The Community Reinforcement Approach* (New York: Guilford, 1995).

5. G. A. Marlatt and J. R. Gordon, eds., *Relapse Prevention* (New York: Guilford, 1985).

Part 2: Program Overview

1. Joseph Nowinski, *The Twelve Step Facilitation Outpatient Program* (Center City, MN: Hazelden, 2006); Joseph Nowinski, *Twelve Step Facilitation for the Dually Diagnosed Client* (Center City, MN: Hazelden, 2011).

Chapter 7

1. Joseph Nowinski, *Substance Abuse in Adolescents and Young Adults: A Guide to Treatment* (New York: Norton, 1990).

2. Joseph Nowinski, *Substance Abuse in Adolescents and Young Adults.*

3. Alcoholics Anonymous, "Bill's Story," in *Alcoholics Anonymous,* 4th ed. (New York: Alcoholics Anonymous World Services, 2001), 1–16; *Alcoholics Anonymous,* "To Wives," in Alcoholics Anonymous, 4th ed. (New York: Alcoholics Anonymous World Services, 2001), 104–21; Narcotics Anonymous, "Who Is an Addict?" in *Narcotics Anonymous,* 6th ed. (Van Nuys, CA: Narcotics Anonymous World Services, 2008).

4. Al-Anon, *Al-Anon Faces Alcoholism,* 2nd ed. (New York: Al-Anon Family Group Headquarters, 1989).

5. Alcoholics Anonymous, "Bill's Story," in *Alcoholics Anonymous,* 4th ed.; Alcoholics Anonymous, "To Wives," in *Alcoholics Anonymous,* 4th ed.

6. Narcotics Anonymous, "Who Is an Addict?" in *Narcotics Anonymous,* 6th ed.

7. Alcoholics Anonymous, *Alcoholics Anonymous,* 4th ed., 104–21.

8. Al-Anon, *Al-Anon Faces Alcoholism,* 2nd ed.

Chapter 8

1. Alcoholics Anonymous, *Alcoholics Anonymous,* 4th ed. (New York: Alcoholics Anonymous World Services, 2001), 105.

2. Alcoholics Anonymous, *Alcoholics Anonymous,* 4th ed., 107.

3. Alcoholics Anonymous, *Alcoholics Anonymous,* 4th ed., 31.

4. Narcotics Anonymous, *Narcotics Anonymous,* 6th ed. (Van Nuys, CA: Narcotics Anonymous World Services, 2008), 18–19.

5. Alcoholics Anonymous, *Alcoholics Anonymous,* 4th ed., 108–10.

6. Al-Anon, *Al-Anon Faces Alcoholism*, 2nd ed. (New York: Al-Anon Family Group Headquarters, 1989), 236.

7. Alcoholics Anonymous, *Alcoholics Anonymous,* 4th ed., 108–10.

8. R. N. Bellah, W. M. Madsen, A. Sullivan, A. Swidler, and S. M. Tipton, *Habits of the Heart: Individualism and Commitment in American Life* (Berkeley: University of California Press, 1985); R. Room, "Alcoholics Anonymous as a Social Movement," in *Research on Alcoholics Anonymous: Opportunities and Alternatives,* ed. B. S. McCrady and W. R. Miller (New Brunswick, NJ: Rutgers University, 1993).

9. Alcoholics Anonymous, *Twelve Steps and Twelve Traditions* (New York: Alcoholics Anonymous World Services, 1952), 27.

10. Bill W., *Tradition Two* (New York: *The Grapevine,* Feb. 1992); original material printed January 1948.

11. Narcotics Anonymous, *Narcotics Anonymous,* 6th ed.

12. Alcoholics Anonymous, "There Is a Solution," in *Alcoholics Anonymous,* 4th ed. (New York: Alcoholics Anonymous World Services, 2001), 17–29; "More About Alcoholism," in *Alcoholics Anonymous,* 4th ed., 30–43.

13. Al-Anon, "Serenity Does Not Depend on Sobriety," in *Al-Anon Faces Alcoholism*, 2nd ed. (New York: Al-Anon Family Group Headquarters, 1989), 91–94; "Living with Al-Anon, We Learn to Live," in *Al-Anon Faces Alcoholism*, 2nd ed., 95–98; "Perfectly Good People Get Alcoholism: A Professional Looks at Her Attitudes," in *Al-Anon Faces Alcoholism*, 2nd ed., 99–101; "The Face of an Angel," in *Al-Anon Faces Alcoholism*, 2nd ed., 102–103.

14. Narcotics Anonymous, "What Is the Narcotics Anonymous Program?" in *Narcotics Anonymous,* 6th ed. (Van Nuys, CA: Narcotics Anonymous World Services, 2008); Narcotics Anonymous, "Why Are We Here?" in *Narcotics Anonymous,* 6th ed.

15. Narcotics Anonymous, *Am I an Addict?* (Van Nuys, CA: Narcotics Anonymous World Services, 1983).

Chapter 9

1. Alcoholics Anonymous, *Alcoholics Anonymous,* 4th ed. (New York: Alcoholics Anonymous World Services, 2001); Narcotics Anonymous, *Narcotics Anonymous,* 6th ed. (Van Nuys, CA: Narcotics Anonymous World Services, 2008); Al-Anon, *Al-Anon Faces Alcoholism*, 2nd ed. (New York: Al-Anon Family Group Headquarters, 1989).

2. Narcotics Anonymous, *Am I an Addict?* (Van Nuys, CA: Narcotics Anonymous World Services, 1983).

3. Al-Anon, "The Face of an Angel," in *Al-Anon Faces Alcoholism,* 2nd ed., 102–103.

4. J. W. Fowler, "Alcoholics Anonymous and Faith Development," in *Research on Alcoholics Anonymous: Opportunities and Alternatives,* ed. B. S. McCrady and W. R. Miller (New Brunswick, NJ: Rutgers University, 1993), 116.

5. Alcoholics Anonymous, *Alcoholics Anonymous,* 4th ed. (New York: Alcoholics Anonymous World Services, 2001), 60–61.

6. Bill W., *Tradition Two* (New York: *The Grapevine,* Feb. 1992); original material printed January 1948.

7. "God, grant me the serenity to accept the things I cannot change, courage to change the things I can, and wisdom to know the difference."

8. Al-Anon, *Al-Anon Faces Alcoholism*, 2nd ed.

9. Al-Anon, "The Nature of Fellowship," in *Al-Anon Faces Alcoholism*, 2nd ed., 231–35; "The Twelve Steps and Twelve Traditions," in *Al-Anon Faces Alcoholism*, 2nd ed., 236–40.

10. Al-Anon, *Understanding Ourselves and Alcoholism* (New York: Al-Anon Family Group Headquarters, 1979).

Chapter 10

1. Al-Anon, *Understanding Ourselves and Alcoholism* (New York: Al-Anon Family Group Headquarters, 1979).

2. Alcoholics Anonymous, *Alcoholics Anonymous,* 4th ed. (New York: Alcoholics Anonymous World Services, 2001), 30.

3. Alcoholics Anonymous, *Alcoholics Anonymous,* 4th ed., 33.

4. Narcotics Anonymous, *Narcotics Anonymous,* 6th ed. (Van Nuys, CA: Narcotics Anonymous World Services, 2008), 21.

5. Mary M., *Family Denial* (Center City, MN: Hazelden, 1985), 4.

6. Al-Anon, "My Brother Is an Alcoholic," in *Al-Anon Faces Alcoholism*, 2nd ed. (New York: Al-Anon Family Group Headquarters, 1989), 170–73;

"Al-Anon Helped Me to Understand My Wife's Problem," in *Al-Anon Faces Alcoholism,* 2nd ed., 147–51; "Other Tools of the Program," in *Al-Anon Faces Alcoholism,* 2nd ed., 246–55.

Chapter 11

1. Al-Anon, *Al-Anon Faces Alcoholism*, 2nd ed. (New York: Al-Anon Family Group Headquarters, 1989), 182.

2. Carolyn W., *Detaching with Love*, original ed. (Center City, MN: Hazelden, 1984).

3. Al-Anon, "Detachment and Growth," in *Al-Anon Faces Alcoholism*, 2nd ed., 31–36; "I Learned to Love," in *Al-Anon Faces Alcoholism*, 2nd ed., 134–39.

Chapter 12

1. Al-Anon, *Al-Anon Faces Alcoholism*, 2nd ed. (New York: Al-Anon Family Group Headquarters, 1989), 236.

2. Al-Anon, "I Belong to Something," in *Al-Anon Faces Alcoholism*, 2nd ed., 113–16; "A Mother of a Teenaged Alcoholic," in *Al-Anon Faces Alcoholism*, 2nd ed., 180–86.

Chapter 13

1. *One Day at a Time in Al-Anon* (New York: Al-Anon Family Group Headquarters, 1990), 54.

2. Carolyn W., *Detaching with Love*, original ed. (Center City, MN: Hazelden, 1984), 5.

3. Al-Anon, "Detachment and Growth," in *Al-Anon Faces Alcoholism,* 2nd ed., 31–36; "Other Tools of the Program—Sponsorship" in *Al-Anon Faces Alcoholism,* 2nd ed., 255–57.

4. Al-Anon, *So You Love an Alcoholic* (Midtown Station, NY: Al-Anon Family Group Headquarters, n.d.).

5. Carolyn W., *Detaching with Love*, revised ed. (Center City, MN: Hazelden, 1994).

Chapter 14

1. Carolyn W., *Detaching with Love*, revised ed. (Center City, MN: Hazelden, 1994); *So You Love an Alcoholic* (Midtown Station, NY: Al-Anon Family Group Headquarters, n.d.).

2. M. Sheeren, "The Relationship between Relapse and Involvement in Alcoholics Anonymous," *Journal of Studies on Alcohol* 49 (1988): 104–6.

3. Al-Anon, *Al-Anon Faces Alcoholism*, 2nd ed. (New York: Al-Anon Family Group Headquarters, 1989), 236.

4. H. M. Tiebout, "Surrender versus Compliance in Therapy," *Quarterly Journal of Studies on Alcohol* 14 (1953): 58–68.

5. Alcoholics Anonymous, *Alcoholics Anonymous*, 4th ed. (New York: Alcoholics Anonymous World Services, 2001), 60.

6. Al-Anon, "A Return to Faith by Way of Al-Anon" in *Al-Anon Faces Alcoholism*, 2nd ed., 125–28.

Index

C

About the Author

Joseph Nowinski, Ph.D., is an associate adjunct professor of psychology at the University of Connecticut and supervising psychologist with Correctional Managed Health Care Division, University of Connecticut Health Center. He has also consulted to substance abuse treatment and research centers at Yale University, the University of New Mexico, and the University of Miami. In addition to *The Twelve-Step Facilitation Handbook* and *The Twelve Step Facilitation Outpatient Program*, Dr. Nowinski is the author of *Substance Abuse in Adolescents and Young Adults: A Guide to Treatment*, and most recently, *Twelve Step Facilitation for the Dually Diagnosed Client*.

Hazelden, a national nonprofit organization founded in 1949, helps people reclaim their lives from the disease of addiction. Built on decades of knowledge and experience, Hazelden offers a comprehensive approach to addiction that addresses the full range of patient, family, and professional needs, including treatment and continuing care for youth and adults, research, higher learning, public education and advocacy, and publishing.

A life of recovery is lived "one day at a time." Hazelden publications, both educational and inspirational, support and strengthen lifelong recovery. In 1954, Hazelden published *Twenty-Four Hours a Day*, the first daily meditation book for recovering alcoholics, and Hazelden continues to publish works to inspire and guide individuals in treatment and recovery, and their loved ones. Professionals who work to prevent and treat addiction also turn to Hazelden for evidence-based curricula, informational materials, and videos for use in schools, treatment programs, and correctional programs.

Through published works, Hazelden extends the reach of hope, encouragement, help, and support to individuals, families, and communities affected by addiction and related issues.

For questions about Hazelden publications, please call **800-328-9000** or visit us online at **hazelden.org/bookstore**.